An expression of amused contempt entered Daros's eyes. 'I felt sure that you were the kind of girl who'd immediately turn to ice if you were kissed unexpectedly. But it would appear that you liked it.'

'Why did you do it?' Her voice was husky and strained.

'It was inevitable. When a man's tempted—'

'I didn't tempt you!'

'Don't be silly. And as I said, you enjoyed it—and you'll enjoy it next time.'

ANNE HAMPSON
currently makes her home in Ireland, but this top romance author has travelled and lived all over the world. This variety of experience is reflected in her books, which present the ever-changing face of romance as it is found wherever people fall in love.

Dear Reader:
Silhouette Romances is an exciting new publishing venture. We will be presenting the very finest writers of contemporary romantic fiction as well as outstanding new talent in this field. It is our hope that our stories, our heroes and our heroines will give you, the reader, all you want from romantic fiction.

Also, *you* play an important part in our future plans for Silhouette Romances. We welcome any suggestions or comments on our books and I invite you to write to us at the address below.

So, enjoy this book and all the wonderful romances from Silhouette. They're for *you!*

Karen Solem
Editor-in-Chief
Silhouette Books
P.O. Box 769
New York, N.Y. 10019

ANNE HAMPSON
Shadow of Apollo

Silhouette *Romance*

Published by Silhouette Books New York

America's Publisher of Contemporary Romance

Other Silhouette Romances by Anne Hampson

Payment in Full   *Man of the Outback*
Stormy Masquerade   *Where Eagles Nest*
Second Tomorrow   *Man Without a Heart*
The Dawn Steals Softly

SILHOUETTE BOOKS, a Simon & Schuster Division of
GULF & WESTERN CORPORATION
1230 Avenue of the Americas, New York, N.Y. 10020

ISBN: 0-671-57064-1

First Silhouette printing March, 1981

10 9 8 7 6 5 4 3 2 1

Shadow
of Apollo

Chapter One

Sylvia was just too beautiful. Hers was a pale, languorous beauty to which men were drawn as if by some magnetic force. That ravishing curve of the rosy lips, the cream skin like alabaster, those enormous innocent eyes, blue as the sky in the full summer of June, that enticing body and those long, slim legs . . . all combined to create an attraction that men found hard to resist. At thirty-two she had become the wife of Frederick Northway and stepmother to his seventeen-year-old daughter, Jenny. Now, at thirty-four, she was widowed and, to her great consternation, heiress to a mere quarter of her husband's estate. Not that the estate was worth very much in any case, because, unknown to either his wife or his daughter, Frederick Northway had gam-

bled so heavily during the last six months of his
life that the fortune for which Sylvia had married him had been lost, so all he left was the
house and furniture and a few thousand pounds
in the bank. Jenny had been left three quarters
of everything, Sylvia one quarter.

Strangely, there was no anger in Sylvia's
reaction; certainly she felt no malice towards
Jenny, with whom she had got along fairly well
right from the start, Jenny's attitude being that
her father had his own future to think about
and, if the entry of Sylvia into his life would give
him happiness, then who was she to raise an
objection?

Jenny had realised, though, as the months
passed, that her father regretted his hasty marriage. Beauty, he once told Jenny, was all very
well, but it was what lay underneath that really
mattered. Sylvia was shallow; her first marriage
had failed because her father-in-law, wise to her
extravagance and mercenary traits, had cut off
his elder son and made his younger son a partner
in his business. Disappointed but resigned, Sylvia had quickly decided that the marriage would
not work, and she and her husband were di-
vorced on quite amicable terms. That was how it
was with Sylvia. She was a good loser. Jenny
knew this, having learned of the woman's personality merely by listening to her conversations
with Jenny's father and with visitors who came
to the house. And now she was not grumbling
too much at all about the will, although she did
remind Jenny that with the law as it stood she
could successfully contest it.

'However,' she added, stretching her long legs

luxuriously as she reclined on the couch, 'for what small amount I'd get it isn't worth losing your good opinion of me.'

'It really makes no difference,' Jenny hastened to assure her. 'You'll live here just the same, because I don't want to see the house—' She stopped to glance inquiringly at her stepmother. 'Perhaps you want to sell, though—so that you can have your share?'

'I've thought about it, darling, and feel I must have time to decide. The house is old, and as it's been sadly neglected it might not fetch very much at all.'

Jenny frowned, her soft grey eyes wandering to the big window and the view across a sweeping lawn to the wooded hills of Dorset beyond. The house *was* old, admitted, and a trifle faded, but, to Jenny, this was where its charm lay. It was lived in, and when Jenny's mother was alive it had known an abundance of love. She had died nine years ago, when Jenny was scarcely ten years old, and the years during which she and her father had lived alone had on the whole been happy ones. Then into Frederick's life had shot the dazzling star that he could not resist snatching. For he was almost sixty, a fatal age for a man, who would, if the opportunity arose, seize the chance of romance, attempting to recapture his youth.

'This house is very attractive,' Jenny pointed out, bringing her attention back to the woman on the couch. 'It's the kind that many people want these days, with the land and the stream and the lovely old woodwork in the building itself.'

'Oh, I do agree to a certain extent, dear,' returned Sylvia languorously, 'but I'm sure we wouldn't get a high price because of all that needs to be done—the plumbing, for instance, is almost archaic, and the electric wiring wants attention. Then the paintwork, and that leak in the library roof . . .' Sylvia shrugged her elegant shoulders and sighed. 'It's a pity dear Frederick gambled the way he did. I wish I'd suspected—but there you are. Men do love having secrets from their wives and children.' She leaned forward to pick up a gold cigarette case from a small table on which there was a large box of chocolates, with the lid off to reveal that the box was half empty, and a gold lighter to match the case that Sylvia had picked up.

Jenny was on a chair by the fireplace, a magazine unopened on her knees. She watched as Sylvia flicked the lighter, then regarded her stepdaughter through the blue film of smoke that floated up before her. 'You know, darling, all our troubles would be over if you married charming David Bransley. He's inherited the entire Bransley fortune in the last year, what with his father dying, and then his uncle, and David being the only Bransley left.'

A pause followed. Jenny frowned into the empty fireplace. 'Couldn't you bring yourself to accept him, dear?' added Sylvia at her most persuasive. 'After all, love doesn't last five minutes, so it isn't as if you'd be missing much.'

Frowning more heavily, Jenny wondered why she found it impossible to dislike this stepmother of hers. But there was something quite appealing about her, something that acted as a shield against people's hurting her. Jenny often lost patience with her, which was natural, yet she scarcely ever voiced even the mildest reproach or criticism. Sylvia was, at heart, a child—a charming, irresponsible, gay and friendly child. The trouble was that those lovely innocent blue eyes so easily filled up, and you felt the biggest heel alive, but this happened only if Jenny disagreed with something her stepmother said or did.

'Oh, how cruel you are, Jenny!' Sylvia would cry in a choked little protest. 'I did so want you to come shopping with me today so that you could help me choose a dress for the dinner-dance tonight. Must you sit there mending that skirt? You could come out with me and buy a new one.'

Or, on another occasion: 'You've upset me, Jenny, and I feel like weeping! I only asked you to lend me your gold bracelet.' It was the bracelet that Jenny's mother had received from Frederick as a wedding present. She was selfish not to lend it, Jenny knew, yet she loathed the idea of her stepmother's wearing it.

Sylvia had stared mistily at her and in the end the bracelet had changed hands. But it had proved to be too small for Sylvia's wrist and Jenny had felt like a hateful cat on being glad that her stepmother could not borrow the bracelet after all.

Now Sylvia was speaking again, recalling Jenny from her reflections. She was talking about David, enumerating his good points and leaving out such minor details as his being a fop and a flirt, and the fact that he was not an inch taller than Jenny and that it certainly wasn't his looks that attracted the girls to his side.

'I detest him!' declared Jenny with feeling when at length Sylvia stopped and hopefully awaited the result of her efforts on David's behalf. 'I wouldn't marry him if there wasn't another man on earth!'

'Nonsense, darling! And that wasn't very original, was it? Now, try to assess the advantages of marriage to David. You'd live at the Manor, while I could have that lovely Dower House. I'd renovate it beautifully, and—'

'Sylvia, you don't need to go on! I am *not* marrying David Bransley!'

A deep sigh of martyrdom escaped Sylvia before she said, in an unfamiliarly petulant voice, 'Then *I* must look around. One of us must marry money.'

'You married Father for his money?' Jenny knew the answer, always had known it, but some impulse made her phrase the question. As soon as she saw her stepmother's changing expression she was sorry, a pang of guilt darting through her, making her want to withdraw the question. How did Sylvia manage it? How did she make you feel so utterly rotten? The big blue eyes had filled up; the pretty mouth moved tremulously. Sylvia stubbed out her cigarette and gave a jerky little sigh that sounded like a sob coming from the very depths of her being.

'How can you accuse me of anything so mercenary! Oh, Jenny, I sometimes think you hate me for marrying your dear father.' A handkerchief—

or, rather, a scrap of snow-white lace—was tremblingly produced and held to Sylvia's eye, while the other was covertly fixed upon Jenny's half-averted face. 'I c-can't answer that b-because I'm too f-full up!'

'I'm sorry.' Jenny rose from her chair, tossing the magazine onto the table by the window. 'I shouldn't have said it. Forgive me.' But her voice was curt, her grey eyes frowning.

'It isn't as if I've come into anything, is it?'

'No, it isn't.'

'I've got practically nothing. It's you who's come into most of what your dear father left. Yet I'm unselfish enough not to consult a lawyer and contest the will—'

'All right, forget it. I've said I'm sorry.'

'But not very graciously,' sniffed Sylvia, dabbing the lace to her eyes. 'Perhaps I should go away, leave you with everything.'

'No, you should not! In fact, you're entitled to half. I'll see the lawyer and have it put right.'

'I won't accept. Oh, Jenny, dearest, why don't you marry David? If you keep on like this he'll find someone else. That's what's worrying me.'

Jenny stared. So that was it! Sylvia wasn't worrying about what Frederick had left simply because she was sure that in the end she could persuade Jenny to accept David's offer of marriage.

'I ought to dislike her intensely, yet I don't.' Standing in her bedroom a few minutes later, Jenny spoke aloud, her eyes drifting to the colour photograph on the table by her bed. Slowly she walked over and picked it up. Her lovely mother. Strange that she could still feel the pain, whereas for her father, who had died only a couple of months ago, she felt scarcely anything at all. They had drifted apart since his marriage, and in the last half-year he had rarely been at home other than to sleep.

Jenny looked down at the face of her mother, the big grey eyes so clear and frank, the mouth a trifle large for real beauty but revealing infinite compassion and understanding. The skin was pale and unlined, the forehead high beneath a halo of shining dark brown hair that waved naturally and curled up at the ends. Jenny moved to the mirror and stared at her own reflection. Yes, her father had been right when he said she was the image of her mother. 'I'm glad I'm like you, darling,' she whispered. If only her mother had lived, Jenny knew for sure, her father would never have gambled away his fortune.

It was less than a fortnight later that Sylvia, having been out to dine with some friends, announced that she had met the most charming gentleman—a Greek whose business was shipping.

'A millionaire!' she told Jenny with a soulful sigh. 'And he's seventy if he's a day! Just think, if I marry him and he dies, I'd probably get millions from his estate! Don't look like that, darling, *please!* I did say that one of us must marry money, didn't I? And as you won't even consider poor David's offer, I'm the one who must do something to get us out of this mess.

Now, don't come that again—' Sylvia wagged a forefinger at her stepdaughter. 'Your expression's so revealing, love. I am *not* going out to work! Yes, you've said that if both of us work it will solve our problems, and you've been out over and over again looking for a job. But you haven't any experience and neither have I, so it's marriage, my love.

'Now, about this gentleman I've met. He's old and can't last long. You read the papers and know just what a wife can get in the way of millions from these Greek shipping magnates. Just imagine if I were to get even one million! And it isn't beyond the bounds of possibility that I could get three or four times that amount!'

'What makes you think he's so very rich?'

'Shipping, my love!' Again Sylvia sighed, this time in a completely ecstatic manner. 'Next to oil, shipping's where the millions are made!'

'This man has no family?'

'Oh, yes, a son and a daughter. The son runs the business from what I could gather. He's thirty-one and seems to be an arrogant sort of man who feels his father needs watching. I expect he's afraid that dear Glavcos will marry and leave his money to his wife.'

'Glavcos? What's his other name?'

'Kyrou, and his son's name's Daros. His daughter has a pretty name, it's Vienoula. They live on the island of Camina. Do you fancy living in Greece, darling?' Sylvia, still in a flowing evening gown and with a mink wrap thrown carelessly over her shoulders, stood with her back to the fireplace in the living-room and eyed

Jenny speculatively. From the depth of her armchair Jenny uttered one brief word.

'No!'

'But you haven't even given it a thought,' protested Sylvia, pouting. How young and vulnerable she looks, thought Jenny, suddenly feeling much older than her nineteen years. It was so hard to avoid going along with her schemes, no matter what your better judgement might tell you.

'I don't intend to give it a thought. Nor should you. These Greeks are awful people—especially the men. You obviously haven't read anything about their way of life. The men are the masters, always. Their wives and daughters are nothing more than chattels.'

'Oh, rubbish, Jenny! How melodramatic can you get? Chattels, in this day and age? I don't believe a word of it. You're just trying to put me off marrying my millionaire.'

Jenny cast her a sidelong glance, noticing the faraway look in her eyes. 'Has this Glavcos asked you to marry him?' she wanted to know.

'Don't be sarcastic, Jenny! I met him only this evening! But I can get a proposal of marriage out of him; you needn't have any doubts about that!'

Jenny had no doubts whatsoever. She had seen the attraction her stepmother had for men. Her very presence in a room made it buzz with the excitement of the male sex; every other woman just looked on . . . with envy.

'When are you seeing him again?' Jenny's grey eyes were questioning, but frowning too, and her mouth was set and stern. That Sylvia had never loved her father was obvious; nevertheless, for decency's sake she ought not to be thinking about other men just yet, much less be avid for marriage.

'On Wednesday evening. He's asked me out to dinner at the Angel. Frightfully expensive, the Angel. He's sending a car for me, as he doesn't drive himself.'

'Sylvia,' protested Jenny, 'you can't really be interested in a man twice your age!'

'Why not?' Sylvia slipped the wrap from her shoulders and threw it down onto a chair. She looked adorable in the dark Edwardian-style blue velvet gown, cut on lines that made her appear no more than twenty-five at the most. Again Jenny felt old. 'He's rich, my sweet! And he's on the verge of falling head over heels in love with me!'

'But you . . . ?' Jenny's eyes reflected censure. 'You don't care a toss for the poor man.'

'Serves him right! "There's no fool like an old fool,"' quoted Sylvia contemptuously. 'He ought to know better, but as he doesn't then why shouldn't I exploit him? If I don't some other woman will.'

'How long has his wife been dead?'

'Four years.'

'His children aren't going to be very happy if he does ask you to marry him.'

'I know it, but what can they do?'

'You might have a difficult time,' warned Jenny. 'I've told you, these Greeks are unpredictable.'

'You believe the son will make things awkward for me?'

'I think that "awkward" is a mild word. He could make things so difficult that you'd come to wish you'd never been so foolish as to marry his father—' Jenny stopped, aware that both she and Sylvia were way ahead of the present situation.

'I'd never regret marrying a millionaire.' Sylvia smiled complacently. 'And between us we could manage this son of his.'

'Between us?'

'You'll come with me to Greece, darling. It would be a chance too good to miss.'

Jenny was shaking her head. 'No, Sylvia. If you marry this Greek it's the parting of the ways for you and me. I couldn't even think of living on someone else's money.' She paused, deliberating on the outcome should Sylvia marry and go abroad to live. She might want her share of the house and the furniture, in which case it would all have to be sold. Well, Jenny felt, she would not be sorry. She must find a job in any case, and she would not want this great house just for herself, even if it were possible to keep it.

'Don't say such things, Jenny. You and I get along so well. I'd not be happy without you now.'

'In that case,' returned her stepdaughter implacably, 'give up the idea of going to live in Greece.'

But after several further dates with the Greek Sylvia was more excited than ever. And, listening to her as she related what had happened, Jenny began to accept the possibility of marriage between this Glavcos and her stepmother. However, after another evening out with him,

Sylvia came home with the information that Glavcos wanted her to meet his children before they talked about getting married.

'I'm a little disappointed in him.' Sylvia frowned. 'I did think he'd marry me and *then* take me over to Greece.'

'It's far better for you to meet his family first,' returned Jenny. 'In any case, you've not known him any length of time. Getting married in a rush is stupid.' But Sylvia had married in a rush before, to Jenny's father. The couple had known one another a mere fortnight when Frederick announced to his daughter that he was thinking of getting married again. Such was Sylvia's effect on him, on all men. She just couldn't help herself.

'I've a feeling that if I don't get married in a rush I shan't get married at all.' Sylvia lit a cigarette and inhaled deeply. 'Glavcos seems a little afraid of his son, yet I don't see why. The business is his and not Daros's. If his son objects to me then he can cut him off!'

Jenny's eyes flew open. 'Cut his own son off! Sylvia, are you crazy? No man would do a thing like that for a woman he scarcely knows!'

'Whose side are you on?' Sylvia's mouth trembled. 'You can be very unkind to me at times, Jenny. And it isn't as if I've ever been unkind to you, is it?'

Jenny bit her lip. As always, a feeling of guilt swept over her when a situation like this arose. 'No, you haven't ever been unkind to me, Sylvia,' she agreed. 'But, really, that has nothing to do with it,' she could not help adding. 'I can't see how I'm being unkind in pointing out something that should be obvious. Glavcos has only just met you, and even though he's fallen head over heels in love with you, you can't expect him to cut off his children simply because he wants to marry you. After all, his son runs the business for him, so it's unlikely that the old man could now manage it himself.'

'You're so practical,' complained Sylvia.

'One of us has to be practical,' rejoined Jenny impatiently. And, after a pause: 'When are you going over to Greece to meet his children?'

'Just as soon as I want to.' She inhaled again, looking at Jenny. 'I'm hoping that you'll come with me—with us, that is.'

'You've told Glavcos about me?'

'Yes, of course I have.' Sylvia rose from her chair and wandered restlessly about the room. 'I told him I wanted you to come with me to Greece.'

'On the visit?'

Sylvia nodded her fair head. 'Yes; I'd like you to live with us when we're married—'

'I've already said I won't.'

'Will you come on the visit?'

Jenny hesitated. For some inexplicable reason, she hated the idea of Sylvia's going to Greece alone—or, rather, with this man Glavcos. There were times when her stepmother seemed utterly fragile and helpless, so vulnerable, unable to take care of herself. From what Jenny had read about Greek men she feared that Sylvia might need protection, or at least some sort of support. Not that Jenny in any way agreed with the idea of her marrying this old man; the whole idea was absurd, mainly because the difference in their ages was far too great. However, it was only with the hope of becoming a widow within a few years that Sylvia was contemplating marriage at all, so perhaps she would resign herself to putting up with certain discomforts for the time being. Jenny glanced at her, watching as she moved with that long-limbed charm of manner, as if she floated rather than walked. It was a pity she set such store by money, deriding love and saying it never lasted. Sylvia could have her pick of the men she met, and it seemed to Jenny that if only she would change her attitude she could marry for love and be idyllically happy.

'I don't know if I really want to come with you,' she said at last. 'You ought to give it thought, Sylvia. You might decide you don't want to marry Glavcos after all.'

'I do want to marry him. I can't be poor, Jenny. It's not for me and you know it. Come! It will be fun; you'll see.'

'Very well; I'll come with you.'

'You angel! I knew you would, though!' Sylvia stopped moving about and lit another cigarette. 'There needn't be any delay. Can you be ready by Thursday or Friday?'

'I expect so,' replied Jenny with a sigh of resignation. *I wonder what I'm letting myself in for?* she added, but silently.

'I'll phone Glavcos and tell him to arrange the flight.'

'How does he come to be in England?' Sylvia

had told her once, Jenny recollected as soon as the question was voiced.

'He came on a visit to friends.'

It was a pity he ever came at all, thought Jenny. Fate certainly played peculiar tricks, disorganising people's whole lives like this.

Within two days everything was arranged. A car came for them and they met Glavcos at the airport. Jenny stared at him, a tall, upright man with very dark eyes and clear-cut features etched on classical lines. Only the mouth was alien to the rest of the face, being weak, loose-lipped and sensual. It seemed to take the strength from the chin, even though the chin was prominent. The man's skin was dark, his forehead lined beneath a shock of straight white hair.

He smiled at Jenny, offering a hand as Sylvia introduced him.

'Glad to meet you.' His voice carried a very noticeable accent. 'Sylvia's told me a lot about you. Nineteen? And very pretty with it. The Greek men'll be staring at you, so be prepared.' But his glance moved to Sylvia and it seemed that already he was jealous of the fact that she would attract many more stares than Jenny ever could.

A uniformed chauffeur was waiting with a car at the airport. A short drive along leafy lanes glowing with hibiscus and oleanders brought them to more hilly terrain, which they entered, climbing through a forest whose bordering trees were beautifully flamboyant, flaring brilliant crimson in the sunshine. Jenny took it all in, determined to make the most of this visit to a land she had always wanted to see—though not quite in circumstances like these!

The house came into view, a magnificent villa gleaming white with pale blue shutters and verandas dripping with flowers. A fountain played to one side of a smooth velvet lawn; statuary and sunken rose gardens, a fantastic shrubbery flaunting every colour, a terraced parterre . . . all combined to give a delightful picture of order and beauty, of wealth and good taste. Suddenly Jenny knew a feeling of tenseness, of apprehension. She wondered why she was here, why she had become involved in the affairs of her stepmother. Sylvia, on the other hand, was cool and full of confidence; Jenny glanced at her and wondered why she had ever thought that Sylvia needed support. Behind her subtly feigned innocence she held a reserve of strength which, decided Jenny, would carry her through the coming ordeal triumphantly enough.

That she herself might be vulnerable and need support never for one moment occurred to Jenny until, a couple of hours later, as she was in the garden, wandering about among the flowers, she found herself face to face with the formidable Daros Kyrou. She had met him on her arrival with her stepmother, but briefly, as he and his father and Sylvia had gone off somewhere to talk in private. Jenny had been shown to a lovely bedroom by a smiling Greek girl, Luciana, one of the three young maids who were kept by the

Kyrou family in addition to the manservant who had admitted them. There were two gardeners, a chauffeur and an elderly man whose occupation appeared to be that of handyman about the house and grounds.

Now, having changed into a pretty sun dress of primrose cotton, Jenny was enjoying the sunshine when she suddenly became aware of footsteps on the path that ran along the other side of the hibiscus hedge. She looked up, and her eyes met those of Daros . . . eyes of steely grey that pierced and probed even while their apparent expression was one of cold arrogance and contempt. Jenny's head tilted automatically; she was not used to being looked at like *that!*

The man strode along on the other side of the hedge but Jenny stood still, angry that her heart was fluttering with apprehension. He reached the end, swung into her path and stopped, a man of towering height, his lithe, lean frame clad in a pair of navy-blue slacks and a white shirt, open at the throat and contrasting startlingly with his burnt-sienna skin. Jenny stared up into his haughty face, her senses alert as if she were preparing for a battle. A most objectionable man, she branded him, a man full of his own importance whose tongue, she strongly suspected, could lash unmercifully. Before her vision rose the statues of Greek gods and athletes she had seen in books and in the British Museum, and she mentally compared the face of this man with those hard, implacable visages of stone. His nobly chiselled features bore such a strong resemblance that he might have been made of stone himself, especially as he was so still and silent, regarding Jenny with unmoving eyes that were so disconcerting that she found herself averting her head, taking the more acceptable course of avoiding his gaze.

He spoke at last, to ask if she were comfortable in her room. She nodded and said yes, very comfortable; and as the room and its bathroom were so luxurious that they could not possibly be other than comfortable, Jenny knew that the words were merely an introduction, an opening for something far less pleasant. And she was right.

Speaking in a voice that carried a profoundly attractive alien accent, Daros said softly, 'Perhaps you and I can have a talk, now that the preliminaries are over. I'm afraid I failed to understand your mother—your stepmother, I believe?' and when Jenny merely nodded, 'The whole story was so incredible as to be difficult to accept. Am I to understand that your stepmother is serious in wanting to marry my father?'

Despite her own ideas regarding Sylvia's ambition, Jenny could not resist answering in a way that would give her intense satisfaction, since it was plain that Daros was exceedingly troubled at the prospect of having Sylvia for his stepmother.

'Certainly she's serious. Why else would she be here? I think it's an ideal match, and I hope there won't be any unnecessary delay with the wedding plans.'

His mouth compressed. 'You think it an ideal match, eh? Well, miss, I can assure you that

there won't be a match. It's clear to me that the
pair of you are interested only in my father's
money and that you'll await his death with the
utmost impatience!'

Jenny coloured guiltily—not on her own ac-
count, of course, but on Sylvia's, Daros's deduc-
tions being only what she had expected—and
lowered her head against his accusing gaze. To
her amazement, and without the slightest warning, he put a hand under her chin and forced her
head up with a jerk that made her feel as if her
neck were being dislocated. She gave a small
cry of pain and protest, trying to swing away, but
he caught her wrist in a grasp that brought
another cry of pain. She stood there, her eyes
filling up, staring at him, noticing the fury in his
expression. This man could be dangerous, she
decided, wishing she had never come to Greece.

'Take notice,' he rasped, his mouth curling
with contempt. 'There'll be no marriage between your stepmother and my father! The pair
of you can go and find some other rich fool who's
outgrown his common sense, because you'll
never succeed in your schemes where my father
is concerned!'

Releasing her, he swung away. She stood
there, trembling, and watched him disappear
from her view. Why, she asked herself, had she
spoken words she did not mean? More important, what had made her act so guiltily when he
was accusing her of being interested in his
father's death? It was Sylvia who was the guilty
one. But Jenny knew for sure that her wily
stepmother would be adopting an attitude of
seraphic innocence; and should Daros speak to

her in the way he had spoken to Jenny, Sylvia would exert every ounce of her expertise and, with tears and protests and all the other devices at her disposal, would probably reduce him to the point where he would come to regard himself as the greatest cad alive.

Chapter Two

A week had elapsed and Sylvia and Jenny had not yet met Vienoula. She was at the University of Athens and would not get home for another fortnight. Daros, meanwhile, had adopted an attitude of cool civility towards both Jenny and Sylvia; he was tolerating their presence in the house and nothing more.

'I'm quite sure,' Jenny was telling Sylvia as they relaxed in two loungers on the lawn, 'that Daros will prevent this marriage.'

'You sound relieved,' accused Sylvia, dropping a careless hand to find her cigarette case, which was on the grass by the chair.

'You know very well that I don't agree with the marriage.'

'Why not?' Sylvia took out a cigarette and put it between her lips.

'It's absurd! An old man of seventy! And you only thirty-four.'

'I can put up with him for a year or two.' Sylvia's tone was complacent. 'And then, my love, a few million from his estate! And that disagreeable son of his gnashing his teeth at having to pay me what's my due.'

'You know,' mused Jenny, looking at her through a haze of blue smoke, 'I never really knew you properly until now.'

Sylvia smiled one of her most winning smiles.

'You sound, darling, as if you don't very much like what you've learned about me.'

A momentary frown darkened Jenny's fore-head, but a second later she was laughing. Sylvia was a wretch, a woman whose sense of values and priorities was all awry, and yet there was something profoundly attractive about her, and it was an attractiveness that had nothing at all to do with her rare and tempting beauty. She might deceive and entice men, but she had an essential good nature and a paradoxical honesty that Jenny could not avoid being drawn to.

'You're mercenary,' accused Jenny at length.

'Admitted, to a certain extent,' was Sylvia's rejoinder. Jenny had almost been waiting to see her eyes fill up and her lovely mouth tremble. 'But why should so many millions be in so few hands? If, by my strategy, I can convert some of those millions to poor, almost starving little Sylvia here, then is there any logical reason for not doing so? After all, you'll be sharing the spoils, Jenny, and can you imagine the time we'll have? When I become the wealthy widow of the Greek shipping millionaire, one Glavcos

Kyrou, we shall begin by having a fabulous house, perhaps in the Bahamas or somewhere equally exotic. We'll book a world cruise on the greatest liner of all time, the *Queen!* We'll buy our clothes in Paris, we'll travel and celebrate and have the time of our lives and—'

'It sounds exciting and wonderful,' interrupted Jenny, laughing in spite of herself. 'And I must say . . .' Her voice trailed away as she noticed her stepmother's changing expression. She was staring over Jenny's shoulder and Jenny turned in quick alarm—to look up into the face of Daros Kyrou. 'Y-you—er—how long . . . ? Jenny's face was scarlet. How much had he heard? Jenny wished with all her heart that she had finished what she was saying, for then he would have heard, '. . . such a life would be nice, but not at someone else's expense. In any case, it would soon begin to pall.'

'Hello, Daros!' Sylvia gave the dark, formidable Greek a look of angelic innocence. She drew daintily on her cigarette and allowed the thin curl of smoke to rise slowly, watching it with her big soulful eyes. 'How wonderful it is out here in the garden! I feel that when your dear father and I are married I shall be spending a great deal of my time here, enjoying this lovely sun!'

Jenny saw his mouth tighten but otherwise there was no change in his expression. She was left guessing whether or not he had overheard all or even part of their conversation.

'You are very sure of marrying my father.' The clipped foreign voice was as devoid of expression as his dark, forbidding countenance. He gave

30

Sylvia no time to answer but swu
in every step he took.

A moment later Sylvia was saying,
have crept from those bushes onto the

'He isn't the kind of man to use stealth in ... der
to eavesdrop.'

'You sound as if he's made a favourable impression on you.'

Jenny shook her head vigorously. 'No such thing. I think he's detestable. On the other hand, you can't blame him for wanting to protect his father, can you?'

Sylvia became pensive, her big, childlike eyes following the tall, erect figure of the man under discussion. He disappeared suddenly, hidden by trees.

'No, I suppose not,' she murmured slowly. 'Loyalty is to be admired. But, darling, has it not occurred to you that it isn't dear Glavcos he's thinking about, but himself? And his sister, of course, who has to have a dowry before she can expect to find a husband. Daros is attractive, don't you think, Jenny?'

The abrupt way in which Sylvia changed the subject threw Jenny and startled her into saying, quite involuntarily, 'You couldn't fall for him, Sylvia!'

The older woman laughed, a rippling laugh that sounded like music drifting over placid water. 'Do you know, darling,' she purred, 'it has just occurred to me that I could fall for him . . . and in a big way . . . ooh . . .' She laughed, this time at her stepdaughter's expression. Disgust and incredulity mingled with bewilder-

ment in those big grey eyes that were always
frank and honest, framed as they were by long,
curling lashes that often sent enchanting shadows onto Jenny's clear, pale cheeks.

'Sylvia,' admonished Jenny severely, 'I'm beginning to think there are hidden depths to you
that are definitely *not nice!*'

'You don't really believe that, my love. I'm
shallow and frivolous but there isn't anything
really wicked about me, now is there?'

Strangely, there wasn't. Sylvia was generous
to a fault: no one would ask for help and not be
given it; beggars were always treated in a way
that made their eyes sparkle and their lips move
in a blessing. Jenny had more than once seen a
suitcaseful of clothes change hands when a
gypsy woman came to the door, children at her
heels.

Jenny knew that if Sylvia were lucky enough
to thwart Daros and marry his father, any
money she might get would not be spent entirely
on herself.

'I can't believe you'd fall for that detestable
Daros,' mused Jenny at length, her eyes on
Panos, one of the gardeners, who was working
on the lawn close to the house, taking out weeds
with a long forked tool. Stocky and very brown,
with a splendid show of gold teeth, he wore the
vraga, those loose-fitting trousers which, Glavcos had told Jenny, were rarely worn these days
by Greek men, especially the young ones. Yet to
Jenny they seemed very practical in this hot
climate. Certainly Panos seemed comfortable
and happy wearing them.

'Daros has got . . . something,' Sylvia was saying in a soulful voice. 'You must admit, Jenny love, that his particular kind of looks are rare.'

'And formidable. Just imagine being married to a man like that!'

'You'd be the envy of every woman who saw you together.'

'He'd be bossy—no, domineering. You'd have to knuckle under the whole time.'

'It could be exciting to be mastered.'

At that moment the man himself reappeared, striding along the patio towards an open window which, Jenny had learnt, belonged to his private room, his study, where he spent several hours each day.

He was undoubtedly an arresting figure of a man, with his unusual height, his athletic gait, his broad, arrogant shoulders and narrow hips. And what an air of confidence! He looked immaculate even though he was informally dressed, the dark slacks accentuating the leanness of his body even as the white shirt accentuated the mahogany of his skin.

Could it be exciting to be mastered? Jenny had never been in love, although she had had several minor relationships. David Bransley had asked her to marry him, and another young man undoubtedly would have done so with a little encouragement—which he did not get. On the contrary, once she saw how things were developing she immediately withdrew and refused to go out with him anymore. She had no idea what she wanted in the man she would marry. All she did know was that love came first, and all else

was of secondary importance. She was an ideal-
ist with an optimistic vision of loving and being
loved till the end of her days. As for what kind of
man she would eventually marry—the mental
picture of him had always eluded her. She did
not even know if she wanted him to be handsome; at one time she had had a preference for
the rugged type and felt she would be at home on
a farm, at another time she had decided the
office type would suit her very well. He would
always be smartly dressed; he'd be intelligent
and handy about the house and garden. . . .

Daros was entering his study via the French
window; he turned instinctively as if aware that
he was being watched. Jenny glanced away but
not quickly enough. She felt annoyed with herself for letting him know that he had held her
attention. When she looked towards the villa
again he had gone and the window was closed.

Jenny rose, restless without knowing why.
'I'm going for a stroll.' She stooped for the book
she had never even opened.

'Come for a swim with me,' invited Sylvia,
stretching her gorgeous legs with a lazy, sensuous motion. 'Dear Glavcos is resting. I asked him
if he swims and he said he used to but not much
now.'

'Don't you care that you'll never have any
proper life together—if you marry Glavcos, that
is?' Jenny stood, book in hand, idly flicking the
pages as she stared down at her stepmother.

'You mean, we won't have the same inter-
ests?' Sylvia's eyes wandered to the window of
Daros's study and a deep sigh escaped her.

'Yes, that's what I mean. In marriage you should both be able to share in the same activities. I'd hate it if my husband couldn't come swimming with me, and play tennis, and take long rambles in the countryside.' Her grey eyes swiftly scanned the immediate surroundings—the lovely gardens alive with colour, heady with perfume; the tall trees of the forest to one side and the orchard to the other; the cerulean sea with a couple of picturesque yachts in the distance; the endless canopy of sapphire above, soft as velvet and bright with sunlight. Not a cloud! And in the garden not a sound other than the drone of insects in the flowers and the whirring of cicadas in the trees. Panos had disappeared and now there was no movement but the gentle swaying of the palms along the seashore and the occasional flash of wings, iridescent in the sun's bright rays.

All was tranquillity. Jenny envied Glavcos and his family—and all the others who lived on the island of Camina, for that matter. She could see other islands basking on the silk-smooth sea, and there were so many more in the Aegean, some barren and scorched by the hot Greek sun, others dotted with windmills and churches, yet each a little different from its neighbours in one way or another. Jenny would like to take a boat and sail to every one, but there would be no time for that on this particular trip.

She mentioned her desires to Sylvia, who shrugged languidly and said, 'Why not, darling? Glavcos has a marvellous yacht. He told me about it and I did have the idea of taking a cruise—just him and me and you . . .' Her lovely eyes moved slowly towards that particular window again. 'I don't suppose your future stepbrother would come with us . . . pity!'

'Future stepbrother?' Funny, but Jenny had never thought of him as that, not as a relation at all. Involuntarily, she smiled. The haughty Daros Kyrou would absolutely hate the idea of such a relationship! Much more would he hate to have Sylvia for his stepmother. Poor man! Jenny could sympathise in spite of her dislike of him. The whole business of his father's stupidity must be driving him to distraction.

'Yes, stepbrother,' repeated Sylvia, smiling. 'Not a bad thought, eh—the wealthy Daros Kyrou as your brother? Something to brag about and be proud of.'

Jenny frowned, wrestling with her impatience. Really, Sylvia was extremely provoking at times! It was not often that Jenny felt like telling her off, but she did have the urge now, although all she said was, 'I'd never even mention the relationship, much less brag about it.'

'You don't approve of my marriage to Glavcos, do you, darling?' Sylvia rose and stretched gracefully, like a feline creature of the wilds.

'You know very well I don't approve! I've said so often enough!'

Sylvia wagged a forefinger at her. 'Your trouble is that you've a conscience—or perhaps I should say that you allow your conscience to trouble you. Put it away, my love! It'll sleep cosily in the far recesses of your mind if only you will let it.'

'You're incorrigible, Sylvia!' Jenny had to

laugh in spite of the severity in her voice. 'I'm off for my walk. See you later!'

'But I want to go swimming!'

'There's nothing to stop you.' From where she stood Jenny could see the curve of the beach and the smooth line where the sea caressed it. 'I want to do some more exploring of this wonderful island.'

'Very well. Mind you don't get lost.'

Half an hour later Jenny was in the hills, watching a lonely donkey pawing the hard, dry ground. It brayed sadly and her heart immediately went out to it.

'If I had the Kyrou millions,' she murmured as she turned away, 'I'd rescue the poor creature.'

She wandered on, coming unexpectedly to a fallen marble column in the middle of a field. She went towards it and found several more. Had this been a shrine in those far-off pagan times when the gods were worshipped in Greece? She strolled about, delighted to discover other relics, one of which was the head of either a Greek god or an athlete. And then a voice made her turn and she saw a young man coming towards her; of medium height, with a clear, bronzed skin and a mass of jet-black hair, he had pleasant features and a friendly smile.

'*Kalispéra!*' he called. '*Pios isthe?*'

'*Kalispéra,*' she returned, then looked inquiringly at him.

'I asked who you were. Are you on holiday?' His accent was more pronounced than that of either Glavcos or his son.

'No; I'm staying at the Villa Camina.'

'You are?' The young man whistled. 'You're a friend of the Kyrou family?'

She had to smile. Already she had learnt of the irrepressible curiosity of the Greeks. They just had to know all about any stranger who happened to appear. She said in a tone of resignation, 'My stepmother's a friend of Mr. Glavcos Kyrou.'

'Mr. Glavcos?' The young man grinned. 'Is she pretty?'

Jenny stiffened, regretting what she had told him. 'I must go,' she said brusquely.

'You not like me to ask questions, no? Pardon! Tell me your name, please. Mine is Helios.'

'Mine's Jenny—Jenny Northway.'

'And you come from England, yes?'

'That's right.' Already she was turning away.

'I go to England one day soon. I come to see you?'

'I don't think so.'

'I have offended you?' He seemed distressed, she thought, and was impelled to reassure him.

'No, not at all. But I've been walking some time and must get back to the villa. It's almost dinner-time.' Which was not strictly true, but she had to shower and change, then the four of them would gather in the sitting-room for drinks half an hour before the gong was sounded.

'I like to meet your stepmother. She is young and pretty, no doubt.' So confident, the 'no doubt'. It was starkly plain to Jenny that Sylvia was not the first woman to find favour with the old man.

She said, suddenly, wanting to learn something, 'Yes, my stepmother is both young and pretty.'

'Mr. Glavcos likes many young and pretty women.' Helios kicked at one of the broken columns. 'Not so Mr. Daros. He does not much care for women.' He paused, looking at her admiringly. 'You pretty, I like the hair that waves and is curling—so!' He actually came forward and touched the ends of her hair. 'I like you for my friend, no?'

'No,' she returned firmly. 'And now, I really must go!'

'*Kali andamossi!*'

'What is that?'

'*Au revoir!*'

'*Kali andamossi.*' She smiled and, turning, went swiftly from the field and back onto the road, her mind on what he had said about Glavcos's fondness for women.

She had not gone more than a hundred yards when she heard a car coming and she stepped aside to let it pass. Daros was at the wheel and to her surprise he stopped and offered her a lift.

'Thank you.' She had wanted to walk but she found it impossible to refuse the lift after he had been considerate enough to stop.

'You didn't decide to swim, then.' His voice was taut, unfriendly.

'No.' She glanced sideways at him as he set the car in motion again. 'Have you any particular reason for saying that?'

'Your stepmother got into difficulties. Luckily I was on hand; I had just come onto the beach with the intention of taking a dip.' His voice was still unfriendly. 'She ought not to swim if she's so bad at it.'

Jenny frowned, opening her mouth to tell him that Sylvia was an excellent swimmer, then closing it again. What was her stepmother up to now?

'What happened? I mean, was Sylvia too far out or something?'

'Not far out at all. In fact, she appeared to be swimming strongly when I first saw her through the window of my study. But as I got to the beach she began to flounder, thrashing about with her arms and crying out for help.'

'You brought her in?' The vision of Sylvia being carried in Daros's arms shot into focus. Fragile and helpless, murmuring husky words of gratitude in that appealing way of hers, Sylvia could actually have been enjoying herself! Immediately on the heels of this thought came a little tinge of guilt. She could be misjudging her stepmother; Sylvia might genuinely have been in difficulties. Certainly Daros thought so.

'Yes, of course I brought her in. She's lying down—or was when I came out about twenty minutes ago.'

'Your father . . . does he know?'

'He went up to her room to stay with her.' Again the voice was taut and his profile in the dimness of the car was dark and stern, with his jaw thrust out and his mouth fixed in a tight, uncompromising line.

Jenny sat there quietly, profoundly aware that this was one of those times when silence was vital. Whatever she said to Daros would be wrong, and therefore she had no intention of saying anything. She just stared at his profile, recalling Sylvia's remark that it could be exciting to be mastered. Well, exciting or not, the woman who was mad enough to marry Daros would certainly be mastered.

Something fluttered along Jenny's spine; she felt bewildered by the way he was affecting her even though he was so silent and coldly indifferent. It was as if he were exuding a special magnetism that made her vitally aware of him as a man. She tried not to look at him, at that set, implacable profile, but the effort of resistance seemed only to heighten her awareness of him. Shaken by her emotions, bewildered by the sensations passing through her, she forced herself to speak, remarking on the beauty of the island and marvelling at the casual way she was able to voice those remarks.

'You like it, then?' Daros did not turn his head, nor did his voice hold any expression whatsoever.

'It's beautiful. I've never seen such lovely flowers growing wild before.'

'The climate's suitable for the growing of exotic flowers and trees.'

'Have you always lived here, Mr. Kyrou?'

'No. I lived in Athens until my grandfather died five years ago.'

'Your grandfather?' she repeated, surprised. 'He must have been very old.' Daros's father was seventy; he must have been sixty-five when his own father died.

'He was eighty-eight.' The merest pause, as if

41

he were making sure that Jenny would be ready to take in his next sentence. 'We're a long-lived family; it's quite likely that my father has another twenty years or so.'

Jenny coloured, remembering that Daros might have overheard Sylvia planning what she would do with Glavcos's money when she was widowed. Jenny said in a rather subdued tone of voice, 'I expect you're trying to persuade your father not to marry my stepmother?'

'Naturally.'

'Sylvia's not nearly so bad as she appears . . .' This was not the right thing to say, decided Jenny, and closed her mouth.

'Are you trying to tell me she isn't a gold-digger?' They were travelling along the coast road, with a fresh, cool breeze sweeping in from the sea and to the right a lush green valley laced with rivulets, its steep sides terraced to grow vines. 'You haven't answered my question, Miss Northway.' Daros's curt voice brought Jenny back from her pleasant appreciation of the scenery.

'I can't answer it.' To her surprise she felt humble and mean and blameworthy. It was as if she were the one who was the gold-digger, who was so mercenary that she would marry for no other reason than to become a rich widow. She ought not to have come here in the first place; it had been her concern for her stepmother that had influenced her, but now she freely admitted that Sylvia was quite capable of taking care of herself.

'The fact that you can't answer it is enlightening enough.' Daros swerved a little to give space to an ambling donkey, heavily laden with vegetables, its owner trudging along beside it. 'Tell me,' he said, when the donkey was safely behind, 'how long has your father been dead?'

She hesitated, again filled with guilt. 'Almost three months,' she answered reluctantly.

'Three months!' He nearly stopped the car in his surprise. 'Only three months—and the pair of you ready to replace him?' His voice was like a rasp, his lips curling in a sneer of contempt. 'I can understand that woman having no love for your father, but you—' He broke off, shaking his head in disbelief. 'What sort of girl are you?'

'My father and I were never close after his marriage.'

'Is that an excuse for forgetting him in less than three months?'

The Greeks, she knew, revered their parents and so she could understand just how he felt. But for her—well, as she had previously realised, she felt more pain for the loss of her mother than for her father, this in spite of the fact that nine years had elapsed since the death of her mother. But then, her mother had been soft and feminine and deeply compassionate and understanding. Her capacity for loving had been as great as that of her daughter and in consequence they had been very close. It was not so with her father. True, they had got along happily before his marriage to Sylvia, but he had always been a hard man where Jenny was concerned, always seeming to adopt the attitude that she could never be a substitute for her mother and so he was wasting his time in trying to show affection. After his marriage he had had very little time for Jenny. The first twelve months had been a great trial for her and several times she had almost left home. But Sylvia was understanding, and kind in her shallow way. Never had she resented Jenny, never had she tried to supplant her stepdaughter in the running of the house. In fact, they got along very well indeed and had been good companions for one another during those last six months of Frederick's life when he had been out every single night and most week-ends, mixing with his pals and gambling away his fortune. That Sylvia might have been the reason for his marked change of habits did occur to Jenny, but she could not accept it as an excuse for what he had been doing.

She was suddenly aware that the man beside her was waiting for an answer to his question and she said quietly, 'I haven't forgotten my father, Mr. Kyrou. I just can't weep for him, that's all.'

He made no further comment but Jenny was not left in any doubt that his opinion of her was now even lower than before.

He turned off, into the town. *Bouzouki* music drifted out from a café at the front of which several dark-skinned men lounged at tables, drinking *ouzo* and playing *tavla*. A white-bearded priest lifted a hand in blessing to Daros as he slowed the car, then stopped altogether, allowing the priest to cross the road.

'*Kalispéra sas*,' said Daros, his lips stretching in a half-smile.

'*Kalispéra*.' The priest's face was calm and

tranquil, his eyes vacant as if his thoughts were lost in the infinite.

The town was left behind; another bearded priest with restless eyes came towards them, his hand lifted in response to Daros's salute. So deeply religous were the Greeks that it seemed impossible that they had once been pagans, worshipping the mighty gods of Olympus.

The afternoon was fading and the sky was bright and clear over the brooding hills towards which they were travelling. There would be a short spell of shadows when the great fiery ball had disappeared over the horizon, but before then would be the incredible glory of a Greek sunset. Every evening Jenny had stood on her balcony, enthralled by a spectacle she would never have believed possible. And now that spectacle was to appear before her eyes again. She leant back and a small sigh escaped her. If only she had come here on her own, on a normal holiday, how very much she could have enjoyed herself!

The car turned into a small road, then entered an avenue of tamarisk trees that was in effect the drive to the villa. Daros was silent; his very manner seemed part of the atmosphere of peace and the miracle of the sunset. To the west the arc of the sky was fading to lavender above the ranks of frilly, gilt-edged clouds; on the drowsy hillsides the shadows had come to transient life under the fibrous saffron rays escaping from the falling sun. Unconsciously, Jenny gave a deep, appreciative sigh just as the car came to a quiet halt outside the front of the house. Daros turned his head and their eyes met. Jenny's nerves fluttered for no reason that she could understand and her heart gave a tiny jerk that was as pleasant as it was disturbing. What was the matter with her? She had never before felt like this in a man's presence.

She slipped out of the car and stood for a space looking towards the west. She said, absurdly, 'Thank you for the lift, Mr. Kyrou. It's . . . it's beautiful!'

He blinked, his eyes interrogating. She coloured daintily, unconsciously lifting a small hand to her cheek.

'I meant the sunset was beautiful,' she explained, rather lamely. 'I was thinking of two things at once.'

He looked down at her for a long moment, an odd expression on his face. It was as if he were puzzled and wanted to ask her a question yet was unable to find a suitable way of phrasing it. After a second or two he turned abruptly and strode away, leaving her to close the car door on her side and make her way to the patio, where steps led up to the balcony of her bedroom.

A few minutes later she was standing just inside Sylvia's room, watching her at the dressing-table as she smoothed cream on her face.

'Hello, darling. Have a nice stroll?'

'Yes, it was fine.' Jenny entered, closing the door behind her. 'Daros gave me a lift back. I hadn't realised I'd walked so far until I saw how long we were in the car.'

'Daros gave you a lift?' Sylvia swivelled around on the stool and stared. 'Did he talk to you? And if so, what did he talk about?'

'He told me of your—er—mishap in the sea.' Jenny took another couple of steps into the room.

'He did?' Sylvia grinned and added, 'I expect he *would* tell you of it.'

'Was it very bad?' Jenny attempted to sound casual but very much doubted if she had kept the sceptical note from her voice.

'Terrible, darling! I thought I was drowning—really and truly. What a miracle that Daros should be there, ready to rescue me! How strong he is, Jenny; you have no idea! I felt so helpless, being carried, just as if I were a baby! And I with practically nothing on. I never felt so embarrassed in my life!'

'You didn't?' Jenny's eyebrows lifted a fraction. 'You sound, Sylvia, as if you enjoyed the experience immensely.'

Sylvia's lovely mouth quivered. 'You don't believe that I was in difficulties. Oh, how horrid of you—'

'Come off it,' broke in Jenny, uncaring if she made her stepmother cry. 'You're a strong swimmer and that sea was as smooth as glass!'

A small silence followed; Sylvia reached out and snapped on another light, this in addition to the two already on, one on each side of the dressing-table mirror. 'Just what are you accusing me of?' Sylvia lifted her eyes to stare directly into Jenny's, her own eyes unbelieving that Jenny should confront her this way.

'I wouldn't put it past you to transfer your affections from father to son,' answered Jenny bluntly. 'You've already said that Daros attracts you.'

'He does, too!' Sylvia's eyes sparkled, then settled down to a dreamy gaze. 'You must admit, Jen, that he's got sex appeal—and then some!'

'He's as cold as stone!'

'Depends on how you treat him. As a matter of fact, I'm beginning to think we shall get along rather well together.'

'Surely you know his opinion of you—of us, I suppose I should say?'

'He thinks we're gold-diggers, you mean? Not anymore—'

'Then he's changed very suddenly. He actually mentioned the expression not half an hour ago, in the car.'

'Accusing me? How uncharitable of him. But he doesn't really hate me, Jenny. I can see that he's going to be putty in my hands.'

'You're optimistic!' retorted Jenny disparagingly. She sat down on the bed, staring out at the last of the sunset, marvelling at the changing colours—the glowing copper-orange and flame, the bronze and saffron and lilac and deep purple. There was even green in the sky, mingling with the filmy threads of rose and palest pink. Stars had appeared to pierce the greys and duns to the east, and the trace of a crescent moon could just be discerned, struggling to bring its argent shape into the swiftly darkening sky. It won at last, as the fiery hues began to die in the west. And soon all the magic of an eastern night would settle over the island and all nature would sleep.

'I've never failed yet, my pet,' Sylvia was saying. 'Just you watch me make Daros fall in love with me!'

'I thought,' said Jenny tersely, 'that you hoped to be a widow very soon. Daros will probably outlive you.'

'I'd not want to be a widow if I married Daros,' she disclosed, reaching out an elegant hand to take up the jar of face cream again.

Chapter Three

There was a brooding expression on Jenny's face as she stood on her balcony, watching the two people laughing down by the fountain.

A week had passed since Sylvia had optimistically announced her intention of making Daros fall for her. Jenny had secretly assessed her chances as nil, since it was a fact that Daros not only disliked Sylvia but was also the kind of man who had the strength to resist her charms. Yet to Jenny's utter amazement he appeared to be very interested indeed in the beautiful woman whom his father wanted to marry. The two had been swimming together several times; they had discussed music and sat alone in the salon and listened to records. They had walked in the grounds, had even motored into town on a couple of occasions when Sylvia had wanted to do some shopping.

And so it would appear that Sylvia was not having much trouble at all in bringing her scheme to fruition. But what of Glavcos? He seemed to have effaced himself for most of the time; at other times he would keep Jenny company, either in the house or in the garden. As for Jenny herself . . . she admitted to being affected by Daros in a way that made his friendship with Sylvia hurt abominably. In fact, she was forced to own that the stings she sometimes felt were actually caused by barbs of jealousy.

She had asked her stepmother how long they were staying on the island but Sylvia was noncommittal.

'Could be for a couple of months or so,' she had answered.

'But we came only to meet Glavcos's family.'

'Well, we haven't yet met his family. Vienoula hasn't been home.'

'She'll be home next week-end.'

Sylvia frowned at her stepdaughter. 'Aren't you enjoying being in Greece, Jenny?'

'Yes, of course. But we didn't reckon on staying here indefinitely.'

'It's not indefinitely.' And that was all. Sylvia had changed the subject and since then had exerted all her energies and charm on the pursuit of Daros.

And it would appear she had succeeded. Daros was smiling down at the beautiful woman from his incredible height while Sylvia was

shining up at him, her lovely mouth tempt-
ingly feminine, with the rosy lips parted
in a most seductive way that was both smile
and invitation. Jenny turned away, aware of
a dragging sensation in the region of her
heart.

She felt it was time she went home. . . .

Daros frowned in surprise and puzzlement
when, in as casual a manner as possible, Jenny
told him she was leaving at the end of the week.

'Leaving? But Sylvia hasn't mentioned anything about it.'

'Sylvia doesn't know.' Jenny had sought Daros
out after seeing him going for a stroll in the
orchard at the back of the villa, and now they
were standing beneath a smooth-leaved orchid
tree, making use of the shade it afforded them. 'I
thought I'd tell you, Mr. Kyrou; it's the polite
thing to do, as you're my host.'

'I'm not your host, my father is,' he corrected
her. 'But no matter about that. Are you telling
me you're going home on your own—without
your stepmother?'

She nodded, wanting to move. He was far too
close; she could smell his after-shave, or perhaps it was body lotion . . . it reminded her of
the elusive perfume of heather on a moorland.
She looked up into his stern face, noting the
attractive contrast between his gleaming white
shirt and the bronzed skin of his throat. The
neck of the shirt was open; she saw a gold
crucifix lying against the dark hair of his chest,
followed the thin chain right up to where it

disappeared, and then she was staring into his face again. Somehow it was a tense moment, with the air around them seeming to be electrified. She thought: If he kissed me it would not be wrong . . .

Naturally she coloured at the thought and naturally he noticed and his straight black brows lifted inquiringly. 'Something the matter?' he asked when she did not speak.

'No. . . .' She was shy and unsure of herself. He was just too attractive, too magnificent, this man who looked like a noble Greek god, so superior, so full of self-confidence. 'No . . . nothing's the matter.'

'I find it strange that you want to go home,' he said.

'I shouldn't have come in the first place.'

'You're telling me that it was Sylvia's affair, not yours?'

She could not answer, could not act with disloyalty to her stepmother. Passing that over, she said quietly, 'Can you arrange the travel for me, please?'

Daros was thoughtful; she knew instinctively that it did not please him that she should leave the villa yet. Please . . . ? Strange that such a word should occur to her.

'I don't think you ought to go home on your own,' said Daros at last. 'In any case, you must discuss it with your stepmother.'

Must . . . Imperious the tone. He had clearly given her an order! Jenny's chin lifted, and there was a sparkle in her eyes as she said, 'I don't have to consult Sylvia regarding my plans, Mr.

Kyrou. I shall tell her I'm going home, naturally, but I don't have to discuss anything with her.'

'Independent, eh? How old are you?' he inquired unexpectedly.

'Nineteen—' She stopped, frowning up at him. 'What has my age to do with it?'

Did he smile? she wondered. She certainly had the impression that he was amused about something. The idea was a revelation in itself as she had not imagined him to be possessed of a sense of humour—at least not where she was concerned; he had treated her with curt unfriendliness right from the start.

'You're young to be so independent,' he remarked, his dark eyes roving her figure very much in the manner of most Greeks. Jenny always felt she was being stripped naked by the moving, all-examining eyes of Greek males. That they were inordinately interested in the female anatomy had been apparent to Jenny from the moment she set foot on the island.

'I'm English,' she reminded him. 'I believe that it's only in Greece that a girl isn't allowed her independence.' A disparaging hint in her voice caught his attention and his eyes glinted momentarily.

'My sister happens to be very independent. However, she is older than you; she's twenty-one.'

Jenny was interested. 'Is she engaged or anything?'

Daros nodded his head. 'She is, yes.'

To a rich man, thought Jenny. Daros would

see to that. 'Will you arrange the travel for me?' she asked again, deciding to change the subject.

'It would be an insult to my father if you cut short your visit.' His eyes had wandered for a moment to a pretty green and pink lizard that had darted onto a stone by his feet. It was now so still as to appear unreal, its head up, its long tail flat against the warm stone.

'An insult?' Jenny tilted her head in a gesture of inquiry. 'I don't know what you mean.'

'In Greece one does not suddenly decide to walk out on the people whose hospitality has been offered and accepted.' His voice was stern and clipped, his accent a trifle more pronounced. Slanting him a glance, Jenny noticed the firmly tensed muscles of his neck and his arrogant chin thrust forward. There was a relentless quality about him that brought a kind of sinking, defeated sensation to Jenny. She knew she wanted to leave here . . . but knew also that if this man decided otherwise then he would have his way.

'I don't want to offend anyone,' she found herself saying almost meekly. 'But on the other hand, I feel it would be wise for me to leave.'

'Wise?' Daros frowned, scrutinising her intently. 'That's an odd word to use, surely?'

She had, in fact, used it unthinkingly. She wondered what his reaction would be were she to own that it was his influence on her emotions that had warned her to leave. 'It was merely a slip of the tongue,' was all she could find by way of explanation.

Daros said, with an odd inflection in his voice,

'What is your reason for wanting to leave, for making up your mind so suddenly?' He was eyeing her narrowly and she had the humiliating conviction that he had guessed she was affected by his presence, by the closeness of him. He was too handsome by far, and even his arrogance was attractive. Jenny had never met any man who had drawn her in the way she was drawn to Daros, and already she had asked herself if these heightened emotions were the prelude to falling in love. There was no doubt at all in her mind that, had he been nice to her, friendly and charming as he now was towards her stepmother, she most certainly would have been in grave danger of losing her heart to him.

'I just want to go home,' she murmured huskily. 'I love it here—please don't think I haven't enjoyed it—'

'But you've had enough? Tell me,' he went on, 'why did you come in the first place?'

'Sylvia wanted me to be with her.'

'She probably still wants you to be with her.'

Automatically Jenny nodded. 'I expect she does.'

'In that case, you had better stay.'

'But—'

'I'll say nothing to my father about your wanting to leave. It would be most painful for him; he'd think you hadn't been happy.' Daros lifted a long brown hand to stifle a yawn. He looked bored all at once . . . but that chin and mouth spelled determination.

Jenny found herself saying, 'I wouldn't like to hurt your father, Mr. Kyrou.' And when Daros said nothing, 'I'll stay for a little while longer, then.'

'Good.' He moved at the same time as Jenny, but she happened to put her foot on a large stone that threw her sideways and she found herself against him, blushing furiously at the contact with his muscled frame and the grip of his hands, which were pressing her arms to her sides so that his fingers were touching her breasts.

'Oh . . . I'm sorry—' Before she could even guess at his intention his hard mouth was pressed against hers, masterful and dominant. She began to struggle, then stopped, her pulses racing in glorious excitement at the thrill of the unexpected as his moist lips slid sensuously over hers, determinedly forcing them apart, and a tremor of ecstasy passed through her at the roughness of his tongue against hers. His hands slid down, their heat searing her flesh through the thin cotton material of her dress, sending waves of fire through her body as he brought it close, melding its contours to thighs as solid as volcanic rock. Everything was forgotten as, for a few sense-drugged moments, she became a willing participant, her eager arms reaching up to twine themselves about his neck, her nostrils catching the musky odour of him, masculine and heady. She felt her stomach muscles tense and then relax as he brought his masculine strength against her pliant flesh, quivered from head to foot as the sensory effects of his ardour were transmitted to her, quickening her breathing, closing her mind to all sense of reality or future regret. A muffled cry escaped her as his hand closed on her breast, warm, possessive and excitingly masterful.

Then, abruptly, she was released and she stepped back unsteadily, a sort of awed wonder pervading her senses because she felt sure that Daros would not have acted like that unless it meant something. But the next moment her cheeks flooded with colour as she noticed the sneer that curled his mouth and the expression of amused contempt in his eyes.

'Well,' remarked Daros suavely, 'that was a revelation and no mistake. I'd felt so sure that you were the kind of girl who'd immediately turn to ice if you were kissed unexpectedly. But it would appear that you liked it.' He was mocking her and she turned away, tears stinging her lids as she shut them tightly, aware of the moisture already glistening on her lashes.

'Why did you do it?' Her voice was husky and strained, her lips quivering because of the bitterness and pain in her heart.

'It was inevitable when you fell against me,' replied Daros coolly. 'When a man's tempted—'

'I didn't tempt you!' she cried fiercely, her small fists clenched at her sides. 'It was an accident, and you took advantage of it!'

He laughed and took her chin in his hand, forcing her head round so that he could look into her eyes, his own flickering strangely, and she wondered if he knew just how deeply hurt she was by what had occurred.

'Do you still want to leave here?' The significance of his words and the way they were delivered brought even more colour to Jenny's face; she felt choked by emotion, was so close to tears that her voice was unsteady when at last she was able to speak.

'I—yes—more than ever now.' She had no idea just how young and vulnerable she appeared.

'But you won't leave,' he told her inexorably. 'You'll stay for as long as I want you to.'

Jenny lifted her chin, eyes sparkling with wrath. 'I shall leave here when it suits me! And that'll be within the next few days!'

'I shall not have my father upset. You've just promised to stay and you'll keep that promise.'

'Things are different now,' she began when he halted her words with an imperious lift of his hand.

'Don't be silly. What's a kiss?' He laughed lightly. 'As I said, you enjoyed it well enough and you'll enjoy it the next time—'

'There won't be a next time!' she flared. I—' Jenny stopped abruptly as she caught sight of her stepmother sauntering along from the house towards the path leading to the orchard. She saw them and increased her pace.

'Oh, there you are, Jenny, darling! I've been looking all over for you.' Her eyes narrowed as she spoke; they slid to Daros, then back, taking in Jenny's flushed face, the brightness of her eyes, the convulsive trembling of her lips. 'Is something the matter?' she asked curiously. 'Jenny—you look distressed.'

'She had a slight accident,' interposed Daros smoothly. 'She stepped on a small boulder and almost fell. It's shaken her, I think, but there's no harm done.' He looked at Jenny, his mocking expression hidden from the beautiful woman who had joined them. 'I should have a rest,' he advised. 'Lie down until dinner-time.'

'Yes . . .' Without looking at her stepmother Jenny turned and left them, wanting nothing more than to be alone.

Half an hour later she was surprisingly composed, having made a firm decision to treat Daros's behaviour as lightly as he did himself. She had no idea by what thought process she had made the decision to stay. All she did know was that she could not go and leave everything clear for Sylvia.

Sylvia came to her later as she sat in her bedroom, trying to read but unable because the words were running into one another.

'Are you feeling better, darling?' Sylvia's purring voice was all concern, her enormous blue eyes searching as they rested on Jenny's pallid face.

'Yes, thank you, Sylvia.'

'What exactly happened?' Gliding over to the window-seat, Sylvia languidly sat down, crossing one sun-bronzed leg over the other. 'I'm sure that Daros didn't tell me everything.'

Jenny flashed her a perceptive glance. She had not lived with Sylvia for over two years for nothing. 'If you're fishing,' she said shortly, 'then don't, because I'm not in the mood for subtleties. What do you want to know?'

Sylvia coloured a little, then pouted. 'That's not very nice, Jenny. You're in a foul mood by the looks of things—'

'I asked what you wanted to know,' broke in Jenny impatiently. 'You've just said that Daros hasn't told you everything.'

'I think,' said Sylvia slowly after a pause, 'that there was more to it than he would admit.'

'I almost fell—Daros, Mr. Kyrou, told you what happened!'

'And it made you as ill as this?' Sylvia's voice was sceptical.

'I am not ill!' snapped Jenny.

After long moments Sylvia purred smoothly, 'I've been thinking, darling, about your not wanting to come here in the first place, and lately it's been very plain that you're getting fed up. So why not go home? I shall be all right on my own—'

'You didn't think so when you were persuading me to come,' broke in Jenny, her narrowed gaze fixed on Sylvia's face. 'Why the sudden wish to be rid of me?'

The blue eyes opened to their full extent. 'Oh, Jenny, what a thing to say!' protested Sylvia, a break in her voice. 'Why would I want to be rid of you, as you so horridly put it?'

'It might be,' returned Jenny tersely, 'that you're afraid of competition.'

'Competition?' Sylvia shook her fair head with well-feigned bewilderment, which did not for one moment deceive her companion. More and more, lately, Jenny found herself seeing a side of Sylvia she disliked, a side she had rarely noticed before. 'Whatever are you talking about? Glavcos would never be interested in you.'

'I'm not talking about Glavcos and you know it! I'm talking about Daros.'

Silence. Sylvia fetched a cigarette case and lighter from the pocket of her dress. 'Had he been kissing you—out there, in the orchard?' she inquired in a brittle voice when presently she had lighted her cigarette.

'Yes, he had.'

Another silence, glacier-cold and long.

It was all too plain that Sylvia was troubled at the idea of competition when she was meeting with such success in charming the man who, at first, had openly despised her. Jenny had no qualms of conscience; on the contrary, she felt that if Sylvia could be convinced that Daros was merely amusing himself with her then she would obviously lose interest and finish with him altogether. And it was reasonable to assume that she could never marry Glavcos and live in the same house as his son. As Jenny saw it, the outcome would be that Sylvia would decide to go home, which was what Jenny wanted, and as soon as possible.

'You actually let him kiss you?' Sylvia's voice bit acidly into Jenny's thought stream. 'Yet you pretended to dislike him.'

'Oh, well,' replied Jenny, determined to adopt a casual mien, 'what's in a kiss? It relieved my boredom and we both enjoyed it, even if Daros and I are not particularly enamoured of one another.'

'You rotten little cat!' exclaimed Sylvia, her

face totally changed by the ugly expression marring it. 'I never thought you'd be such a—a viper!'

'Make up your mind, Sylvia,' she flung back. 'Either I'm a cat or I'm a viper; I can't possibly be both.'

'Don't be frivolous!' ground out Sylvia from between her teeth. 'You're rotten and I wish with all my heart I hadn't brought you with me!'

'Daros,' said Jenny quietly, 'is a philanderer. He's playing fast and loose with you!'

'Liar! You tempted him!' She rose and came towards her.

'Then he was darned easily tempted. I merely stumbled and the next thing I knew he was in a rare passion!'

'A passion?' echoed Sylvia incredulously.

'All Greeks are passionate; you don't need me to tell you that.'

'Did he—he—make . . . ?' Sylvia's voice trailed off. She looked as if she were ready to burst into tears.

'Make love to me?' Jenny hesitated, then decided she could not go as far as that. 'No, he didn't . . . but he might next time.'

'I don't believe you'd let him!'

'It all depends where we are. I might not be able to make my escape!'

'Shut up!' Sylvia actually stamped her foot. 'You're laughing at me!'

'No such thing.' Jenny paused, then added in an expressionless voice, 'I can't understand why you're so against my having a little fun with Daros. After all, it's Glavcos who's your boy-friend, not his son.'

Sylvia gritted her teeth. 'You know very well that it's Daros I want now. I told you it was!'

Jenny shrugged her shoulders. 'Well, if you want to marry a rake, a philanderer, then go ahead. I can't say I'd care for that kind of life myself—my husband having dozens of pillow-friends.'

'He wouldn't—'

'But he would,' argued Jenny with far more patience than she felt. 'You've had proof that he's no good.'

Sylvia looked at her with sudden suspicion. 'What's your little game?' she demanded harshly. 'It's not like you to play around with a man, letting him get fresh with you. Just what are you up to? Tell me!'

'I can't convince you, can I? So we might as well let it drop.'

'No, we won't. You're going home!'

Jenny shook her head. 'No, Sylvia, I'm not. Life has just begun to be exciting. I have as much right as you to a bit of fun—'

'I'm *not* getting any fun!' Without warning Sylvia burst into tears, her whole manner changing as she quavered, in a voice that was so very familiar to her stepdaughter, 'Oh, Jenny—h-how c-can you be so unkind to—to me? I never thought you'd t-take my boy-friend from m-me—' Another burst of weeping, which left Jenny coldly unaffected. 'Go h-home—*please*, and let m-me get Daros b-back.'

'Back?' with a lift of Jenny's eyebrows. 'You've never had him so how can you get him back?'

'You're heartless!' wailed Sylvia, catching her breath in a choking little sob that seemed to leave her bereft of speech. She sought for the usual wispy scrap of white lace and put it to her eyes.

'Here—!' Jenny threw her a proper handker-chief. 'For heaven's sake, Sylvia, stop this child-ishness! I'm not going home and I'll do what I want to with Daros and that's that!'

Chapter Four

That evening they all went out to dinner, to a restaurant on the seashore. The dining area was a long, wide veranda jutting out from the main building, and seemed to be resting on the rocks. It was, therefore, right out over the sea, shaded in the daytime by trellised vines that formed a delightful cover. In the evenings, coloured lights hidden in the vines provided a fairy-tale–like glow, but there was added illumination provided by the candles set in crimson glass chimneys on each table.

The table had been reserved and was right at the front and in one corner—undoubtedly the best position in the restaurant. Glavcos, looking a little staid in black with a white shirt and bow tie, held Sylvia's arm possessively, guiding her to a chair and standing by her as the waiter drew it out for her and shook out the napkin. Daros, superb in a pearl-grey linen suit that was not quite evening dress but certainly not what would be worn during the day, indicated the chair Jenny should occupy, which was opposite his. She sat down, marvelling at her calm as she sent him a glance from under her lashes. And she caught her breath. The shirt he wore was frilled down the front, pale blue with darker blue edging on the frill. His black hair, thick and straight and shining, was brushed back from his forehead, but a few strands, teased by the breeze, had fallen out of place onto his brow, adding to his attractiveness. Aware of her gaze, he curled a sardonic lip and she instantly looked away. Glavcos and Sylvia were talking quietly while Jenny and Daros just listened. Then, soon, they were looking at each other, Daros's eyes filled with mocking amusement and Jenny's glinting with fire.

The waiter appeared and drinks were served, followed by the first course of lobster and avocado pears. Succulent kebabs came next, accompanied by a tossed green salad. The air around was balmy; atmosphere was created by *bouzouki* music being played by four musicians somewhere just inside the main building. Three men in gaily coloured costumes took the floor and danced the lively *kalamatianos*, their bodies moving as if on springs.

'Isn't it marvellous!' Sylvia's voice was a delightful purr, like the sigh of a breeze at night. Her smile was alluring, her big baby eyes wide and innocent as they sought and held Daros's dark, unfathomable gaze. Jenny felt completely out of place, an intruder who had inadvertently stumbled on a couple of lovers.

She looked at Glavcos but he was watching the dancers and she heard him say, as if to himself, 'It seems only yesterday that I could do that, and more!'

And then she saw Helios, coming onto the veranda with two other young men.

Jenny smiled and said, in answer to his spontaneous greeting, 'Kalispéra, Helios. How nice to see you again.'

His eyes brightened in surprise; plainly he had not expected such enthusiasm. 'You are enjoying the dinner, yes?'

'Very much.' Jenny spoke to Sylvia, introducing her to the young Greek, who, all smiles, in turn introduced his friends. Both Glavcos and Daros knew the three, who were natives of the island. Glavcos spoke a few words to them but his son merely nodded, his eyes on Jenny's face.

'How do you come to know Helios?' he asked her when the others had gone.

'I met him when I was out walking.'

'You weren't introduced?'

'No . . . we just met and—and talked.' Her colour rose, tinting the high cheek bones and accentuating the delicate contours of her face. 'You obviously don't approve.' She noticed that both Sylvia and Glavcos had stopped eating to give their whole attention to what was going on between Daros and herself.

'I certainly do not approve of a young girl

picking up a strange man and chatting with him.'

'Picking up!' exclaimed Jenny, her eyes suddenly blazing. 'What a crude expression to use, Mr. Kyrou!'

This was not a situation she would have wanted, not with Sylvia sitting there to witness the disharmony between Daros and herself.

'Did you really pick him up, dear?' inquired Sylvia, pretending to be shocked, but Jenny, with her wide experience of her stepmother's ways, realised at once that she was being disingenuous; she would exploit this situation to blacken Jenny in Daros's eyes. 'It isn't like you. But I must admit that he *is* rather good-looking, and he has the pleasantest of smiles.'

'I didn't pick him up!' Jenny was so furious that she found herself adding, 'But even if I did it has nothing to do with anyone here!' There, she'd been outright rude but she didn't care. Even the quick lift of Daros's eyebrows could not disconcert her.

He said softly, 'While you are a guest in my house, Miss Northway, you are automatically under my care. Therefore, you will not take risks . . . none whatsoever. Do you understand?'

'Risks?' Jenny was flustered now. She'd been scolded and it hurt.

Noticing her embarrassment, Glavcos came to her rescue. 'Daros is merely pointing out that, in Greece, a young girl staying with a family is automatically under the control of the master of the house. In effect, it is his duty as a host to see that no harm comes to his guests, and this

applies particularly to young unmarried females.'

'He told me you were my host,' she returned.

Glavcos shrugged. 'It is my house but Daros is
in full charge,'

Making no comment on that, Jenny merely
said, 'I think I can take care of myself, Mr.
Kyrou.'

'Of course you can, darling,' interposed her
stepmother soothingly. 'Daros, you have no need
to worry about Jenny. She might indulge in a
mild flirtation, but she's not one of these preco-
cious modern females who would be likely to let
you down by committing some really serious
indiscretion—'

'Sylvia,' cut in Jenny sharply, *let the matter
drop!*'

By this time Jenny was hot with embarrassment and furious with Sylvia. She wanted to get
up and walk away from the table.

Daros, his eyes implacable, ignored her heated
request to Sylvia as he said, still in that same
soft tone of voice, 'I asked you, Miss Northway, if
you understand my order that you take no risks.
You haven't answered me.'

'Order!' ejaculated Jenny, outraged and hearing this one word above all the others. 'Mr.
Kyrou, I do not let anyone give me orders!'

A white-coated waiter was hovering close by,
ready to serve the dessert, a compote of spiced
fruit with fresh whipped cream and walnuts. He
was interested in all that was going on and had
no intention of missing anything. Daros lifted an
imperious hand and waved him away, then

looked at Jenny, waiting for her answer. She remained stubbornly silent, hating Daros with a black venom for goading her into causing a scene like this at the dinner table. She heard him repeat, in tones even quieter than before but carrying a warning that she was quite unable to ignore, 'Do you understand, Miss Northway?'

Jenny gulped to release the ball of anger that was blocking her throat. 'Yes, Mr. Kyrou,' she answered almost inaudibly, 'I understand.'

Without another word Daros beckoned to the waiter, who served the sweet course while another waiter poured the Asti Spumante to go with it. Glavcos glanced at Jenny in a sympathetic way that served as balm to her wounded pride. And a short while later, when Daros had taken Sylvia onto the floor, he asked her to dance. She rose at once, swinging into his arms, her eyes seeking the couple who were attracting all the attention not only by their appearance but by the superb manner in which they danced together.

'They make a most attractive couple, don't they?' Glavcos had followed the direction of Jenny's gaze and he spoke without rancour. 'My son is a remarkably handsome man, don't you think?'

Jenny, in no mood for agreeing with Glavcos but heeding her manners—somewhat belatedly!—said yes and changed the subject. Glavcos laughed, looking at her and shaking his head.

'He's riled you, Jenny. He always riles women sooner or later, and no wonder, with that high-handed manner he adopts towards them.' His eyes slid to Daros, who was holding Sylvia rather more closely than was necessary. 'I expect he'll change his ways when he finds the one he wants to make his wife.' So emotionless the voice. Not a sign of anger or pique that his son was, quite openly, taking over his girl-friend!

'I don't think I could ever get used to the way your people treat their women,' said Jenny. 'In England we have equality of the sexes.'

'It sounds very well on the surface,' he mused, 'but tell me, Jenny, do women really want to be the bosses?'

'They're not the bosses,' she protested. 'They're equals.'

'Greek girls like to be mastered by their husbands.'

'Would you master Sylvia?' inquired Jenny curiously. She was recalling what her stepmother had said on this subject.

Glavcos smiled faintly before producing an answer. 'I'd never want to master Sylvia, no.'

The music stopped and the four returned to their table to sit chatting for a while over their wine. When the band struck up again, playing a waltz, Daros surprised Jenny by inviting her to get up. She would have refused had it been at all possible; instead, she rose stiffly and slipped into his arms.

He danced superbly; Jenny was also a good dancer and as they progressed around the un-crowded floor she gained confidence, feeling she was not as inferior to Sylvia as she had always believed. She supposed her feeling of inferiority had stemmed from the fact that Sylvia's dancing had been repeatedly praised in Jenny's hearing.

As the silence stretched between them Jenny became uncomfortable. Why didn't Daros speak to her? He seemed totally indifferent and she supposed that his gesture in asking her to dance had been no more than a punctilious observance of duty. The idea angered her out of all proportion; she would have liked nothing better than to have left him in the middle of the floor, just to give his intolerable pride a crushing jolt!

The moments ticked away and still he maintained his silence. Jenny believed he would have maintained it throughout the entire dance had he not been hailed by someone he knew who was sitting at a table in a secluded corner, well away from the lights. The man spoke in Greek and as Daros answered in the same language Jenny had no idea what was being said. However, Daros introduced her to the man and his wife, speaking, naturally, in English. The couple, in their early thirties, were Costa and Maria Diakos, who were on holiday, having come from Athens, where they lived. Costa was in shipping and Jenny soon gathered that he and Daros were business acquaintances.

'Sit down a moment,' invited Costa, smiling to reveal some very impressive gold fillings. He had a fat cigar in one hand and worry beads in the other. His wife, very dark and slim, was smoking a cigarette from a long, gold-embellished holder. 'I was intending to try to see you tomorrow, Daros, on some business matter. Shall you be at liberty in the afternoon?'

Daros nodded. 'Yes, of course.'

'How is your father? He was looking fine when I saw him in Athens a few months ago.'

'He's in excellent health, Costa, and will be around for a long time yet.' Daros's glance flickered to Jenny, its significance causing her to colour guiltily. 'I'll tell him you were asking about him. He's here tonight, as a matter of fact.'

'He is?'

'Yes.' A small pause and then; 'He's with a lady friend of his. Miss Northway's her step-daughter. They've come from England.'

A swift, amused glance passed between Costa and his wife; it went unnoticed by Daros, who, rising, said something in Greek before moving away with Jenny as she too rose and said a brief goodbye to the couple. More dancers were on the floor by this time and, owing to the lack of space, her partner several times had to bring Jenny close to him in order to avoid collisions with other couples. She could feel his strong, muscled strength against her own soft and supple frame. Their bodies seemed to meld together as if it were both her intention and his that they should. Angered by the thought, Jenny strained away from him. He looked down at her in amusement as the colour rose to tint her cheeks. 'We're becoming a bit hemmed in,' he said, the faint accent carrying a satirical note. 'Perhaps you'd rather we gave up?'

She averted her head, aware that her cheeks were burning. It was incredible that he could be so undiplomatic, but she knew for sure that he was enjoying her discomfort. Hateful man!

'Yes,' she returned without hesitation, 'I would.'

'A pity,' he said unexpectedly. 'I was enjoying our dance.'

'You amaze me,' she snapped, furious that he was mocking her.

His straight black brows shot up in surprise at the sharp, unfriendly tone of her voice. 'You don't believe me?'

She decided to be frank and say what she thought. 'You danced with me simply because you considered it your duty.'

They were walking off the floor and had come to the edge, the space between the dancers and the dining-tables. He stopped, compelling Jenny to do the same.

'You take a great deal for granted,' he returned shortly.

Jenny hated the idea of voicing an apology, but felt obliged to do so. 'I'm sorry if I made a mistake,' she murmured, wanting to walk away, back to their table, but Daros remained where he was and she could hardly brush past him.

'Tell me,' he said, 'what have you got against me?'

She shot him a glance, eyes kindling. 'Plenty! Have you forgotten what happened a short while ago? You deliberately humiliated me!'

'You deserved it all,' he returned with infuriating imperiousness.

'And you kissed me,' she snapped, then felt extremely foolish for mentioning that.

'And you reciprocated.' His alien voice held a distinct element of humour and Jenny averted her head, blushing.

'You took me by surprise,' she began, then stopped, uncomfortably aware of the weakness of her statement. Daros was laughing softly and she felt she hated him even more for making her feel small. 'We can't stand here,' she snapped, noticing several couples coming onto the floor. 'We're in the way.'

'All right; we'll go outside.'

'No—' Again she stopped, her eyes catching sight of Sylvia, who was glowering at her from their table at the other side of the dance space. If she were to prove to Sylvia that Daros was a rake then she had better begin as soon as possible. Making sure that she and Daros still held her stepmothers's attention, Jenny flicked him a coquettish glance and said archly, 'Where shall we go?' Actually, she was trembling at the idea of going out there with him into one of the many dark places.

His eyes widened in surprise, then narrowed suddenly; he slid a glance in Sylvia's direction, his lips pursed. A long, unfathomable moment passed before he spoke. 'I'll show you.'

Taking her arm, he led her away from the lights and music and chatter, following a pathway leading to a remote part of the gardens where a small copse provided the darkness that Jenny now wanted to avoid.

There was a little seat round the trunk of a tree and he told her to sit down. 'You'll probably feel safer that way,' he added in tones edged with mockery.

'What do you mean by that?'

'You look scared out of your wits.' Daros sat down beside her, close but not touching her.

76

'What's your little game?' he demanded unexpectedly.

'Game?' Surely he hadn't guessed what she was about! 'I don't know what you mean.'

'Leave it,' he said impatiently. 'I asked you what you had against me.'

'I've already told you.' She paused, aware that if she were to carry out her resolve to cause a rift between him and Sylvia, then she ought to be assuming a placatory attitude towards him. 'I suppose it's nothing really serious, in retrospect,' she added, with assumed self-deprecation in her voice.

'Yet from the first you've adopted an attitude of hostility towards me.'

'I didn't start it,' she protested indignantly. 'You decided right at the beginning that I was mercenary and grasping, which was a harsh judgement seeing that I hadn't given you any cause for reaching such a conclusion.'

Daros turned his head and although she could not see his expression in the darkness she sensed intuitively that his eyes were narrowed and accusing. His next words left her in no doubt that her assumption was correct.

'Let's stop prevaricating, shall we? I overheard you and your stepmother planning what you would do with my father's money when he was dead.'

Jenny turned away—so abruptly that the action must seem to prove her guilt. If only she could explain, she thought unhappily, convince him that she was not mercenary, not in the least interested in his father's money. She realised that she wanted him to change his opinion of

77

her, to come to regard her as a *nice* girl—which was all most illogical seeing that her main aim was to get away from Camina as quickly as possible.

'I don't wish your father dead, Mr. Kyrou.'

'No?' with a certain scepticism that could not possibly be missed. 'Well, let's not waste any more time in this kind of unprofitable talk,' he added decisively. 'I said you looked scared, but, after all, you'd not have come out here unless you wanted me to make love to you—'

'I—I—' she broke in, then floundered.

'*Why* did you agree to come out here with me, Jenny?' inquired Daros curiously.

Jenny . . . Only now did she own that she had longed to hear her name on his lips. It rolled off them, faintly accented, in the most attractive way.

'Well,' he prompted, 'what was your reason?'

She turned to him, wishing she could see his face, read its expression, for she was again wondering if he had guessed what she was about. It would not strike her as surprising simply because she had accepted right from the beginning that he was a man of quite extraordinary perception.

'What makes you suspect there's any reason other than—than—' She stopped, fervently thankful for the friendly darkness that hid her rising colour.

'That you wanted me to make love to you,' he finished with callous disregard of her feelings. He was laughing at her, she was sure, and somehow his mood was attractive . . . drawing her against her will. He was dangerous to be with . . . but exciting. And the night was exciting too, the balmy, perfumed air like silk against her face, the drift of music from the café a haunting complement to the atmosphere of romance. Jenny's heart quivered; he had managed to come closer without her even realising it, and she was vitally affected by his nearness. The after-shave she had noticed when they were dancing took on a difference now, reminding her of the wild heather moors of Derbyshire where she had spent a holiday once with her father, before Sylvia came into his life to dazzle his senses and to lead his daughter into a situation such as this.

'What are these quiet meditations that are so absorbing?' Daros's voice was soft and vibrant, his mouth so close to her face that she could feel his cool, clean breath caressing her cheek like a summer breeze.

'It was nothing.' Her voice sounded husky; she hoped it did not betray her heightened emotions. 'I was thinking about Father and a holiday we took in Derbyshire—' She shrugged self-deprecatingly. 'I don't expect you've ever heard of it.'

'I have, but I've never been there.'

'No. I expect that if you've been to England you merely visited London.'

He countered, 'Why should you assume a thing like that?'

'Because every foreigner who visits England makes for London by the quickest route. Then they go home and say they've been to England. Well, they haven't. London is not England any more than Athens is Greece.'

A hint of indignation rose within her voice and caused Daros to smile and say, 'Obviously you don't come from the London area.'

'I come from the north of England, and that includes such counties as Cheshire and Derbyshire and the Lake District. If only visitors would take a few tours to other parts of my country they'd discover wonderful places and people.'

'And you consider Sylvia and yourself to be wonderful people?' inquired Daros with a curious expression.

'You don't know everything!' was all Jenny could think of saying to that. She could scarcely exonerate herself when he had overheard the conversation to which he had referred just now.

'You sounded like a pair of gold-diggers that day.'

Again deflated, as no doubt he meant her to be, Jenny fell silent, reflecting soberly on the assertion he had made. If his opinion of Sylvia had not changed, then why had he shown so much interest in her lately? Sylvia had been rapturous about it, had even gone as far as to allow her thoughts to dwell on the possibility of marriage to Daros instead of to his father.

'I've gained the impression that you were beginning to like my stepmother.' Jenny spoke her thoughts aloud, almost unconsciously.

'As a man,' returned Daros with amused mockery, 'there is a great deal about Sylvia that I like. She has everything—looks, figure and sex appeal in plenty.'

Jenny passed her tongue over lips suddenly gone dry. What price her plan if Daros was already feeling like this about Sylvia? Was genuinely attracted to her?

'You—you w-wouldn't marry her?' The thought was too unbearable. Jenny felt she would never be happy again if Sylvia were to gain her ends and marry Daros.

'I could,' he murmured, eyeing Jenny thoughtfully. 'Yes, it's possible.'

She shivered, cold and empty. A tense silence fell, a painful silence for Jenny. She was so conscious of the hollowness in the pit of her stomach that she involuntarily pressed her hand against it, a movement that obviously did not escape her companion, because he asked her if she were feeling unwell, his arm encircling her as he spoke, bringing her close to the granite hardness of his chest.

'I'm fine,' she answered, vainly struggling to pull away. 'If you're in love with my stepmother, then why are you here with me?'

'I haven't said I'm in love with her—'

'But you're contemplating marriage to her,' Jenny broke in swiftly. She wanted nothing more than to get away, to be alone. For although for the past few moments she had been trying desperately to suppress the knowledge that was forcing its way into her mind, she found it impossible. She was madly in love with a man who was not only a philanderer but who was also contemplating marriage to her beautiful stepmother.

'A Greek doesn't trouble himself about love,' Daros was saying casually. 'It's enough for him that his wife possesses the physical qualities that will satisfy him.'

So cold and clinical! His whole manner seemed totally at variance with his obviously passionate nature.

'You hated the idea of Sylvia's marrying your father, yet you would marry her yourself?'

'She wanted to marry my father for his money. And it may interest you to know that she isn't the first by any means. My father needs protecting from women such as Sylvia, and it is my intention to protect him.'

An astute guess was born in Jenny's mind as a result of his words. 'Is that why you're marrying Sylvia—to save your father from her?'

'First, you are running ahead of the situation,' he told her suavely, withdrawing his arm and resting his back against the seat. 'I haven't actually said I intend marrying Sylvia.' He paused, and Jenny had the strange impression that his next words were merely a casual addition. 'As I have said, Sylvia has sex appeal in plenty. She'd be wonderful in bed.'

Jenny coloured up, again thankful of the darkness that hid her embarrassment. 'Is that all you think about?' she managed, surprising herself.

'What else is there to think about in marriage?'

'Love,' she answered briefly, and his laugh was like a rasp on her nerves.

'Women's stuff,' he mocked.

'You're cynical and hard,' she accused. 'Men do fall in love, no matter what you think!'

'More fool they. They live to regret it.'

'You're going to miss a lot in life,' she warned,

82

unhappily aware of the weight on her heart. 'What about the spiritual side of marriage?'

'Idealism, nothing more.' The mockery was still there.

'You're trying to say it doesn't exist?'

She sensed his frown as he replied, 'Don't let us get too deep, Jenny.'

'You're avoiding the issue.' What was she trying to do? Jenny asked herself. The man was hard and unemotional; to suppose that beneath the veneer existed something warm and sensitive was utterly absurd. And yet . . . At times he seemed different, when she had watched him in the garden, for example, picking a rose that he put between his teeth, then walked on again, his head forward as if he would smell the perfume more easily that way. And she thought about the gold cross he wore on a chain around his neck. . . .

'What are you thinking about?' he asked, bypassing her comment.

'You,' she replied frankly.

'Yes?'

'You puzzle me at times.' Her voice was low and pensive, a sigh in its depths that did not escape him.

'In what way do I puzzle you?' He sounded interested and patient.

'Sometimes you're so cold and—and haughty—' She paused. 'I suppose you're offended by my saying that?'

'I'm not offended quite so easily,' was his smooth denial. 'Please continue.'

'At other times you're—different.'

'No one can be cold and haughty all the time.'

'You're laughing at me!'

'Let's change the subject, shall we? We were talking about Sylvia, and the fatal charm she has for men.'

Fatal charm . . .

'What about your father? How is he going to feel when you're married and living in the same house with him?'

'I've just said you're running a little ahead of the situation.' The strange inflection in his tone baffled her, bringing a frown to her wide, intelligent forehead. Was he playing with her, amusing himself at her expense?

'I see nothing rational in marrying without love. . . .' Her voice trailed off into silence as she again asked herself what she was trying to do.

'Are you suggesting it would be irrational for me to marry a woman as beautiful and appealing as your stepmother?' Something intangible in his tone brought back the idea that he was playing with her, but she was too dispirited to make an attempt to fathom it. And after a moment she stirred restlessly, deciding to end this conversation before it became too involved for her.

'I want to go back,' she said querulously. 'Please take me.'

'Now?' She felt him stiffen in surprise. 'We came out here to make love—'

'We did not! I want to go back!'

'All right,' he agreed, much to her surprise. But as soon as they were on their feet he had her in his arms, her lips ruthlessly crushed in a kiss that left them swollen and bruised and her temper flaring. She struggled frantically, actually managing to slap his face before her hands were caught in a vise-like grip that brought a quivering cry of pain to her lips.

'Vixen!' His smouldering voice was the danger signal for what came next as, her arms now trapped against her sides, she was swept into a vortex of passion that made her wonder if Daros were a throwback to the pagans. Pagans. Men whose brutality was commonplace in ancient times when, with their barbaric power, they annihilated every enemy that crossed their path. His treatment of her was nothing more nor less than a savage, arrogant taking of all he desired, his kisses fierce and brutal, his sensual mouth dominant and cruel, his insistent hand in the small of her back forcing her body to fuse with the whipcord hardness of his, igniting flames that reached out to every part of her, affecting her nerves, evoking abandoned responses that brought a little laugh of sheer triumph to her captor's lips. By the time the storm of his passion had stilled itself Jenny was totally spent, her small hands clinging to him, her exhausted body limp within the support of his arms.

After what seemed an eternity of silence and immobility Daros released her, sitting her down as if he doubted her ability to stand on her feet.

'We'll go back whenever you're ready.' His voice, even and controlled, made such a startling contrast to the primitive outburst of his passion that Jenny gasped in disbelief. How could he be so cool and unaffected when she herself was trembling from head to foot, her nerve-ends ragged, her heart thudding with almost painful intensity?

But at length she became calm in body if not in mind. She rose from the seat and stared up at him, his profile a dim silhouette, vague and softened by the darkness.

'I'm ready now,' she said, marvelling at the calm dignity with which she was able to voice the words. 'I hope we haven't been away too long.'

'Not too long at all,' smoothly, and with a distinct note of mocking amusement in his deep-toned foreign voice. 'It's amazing what can be done in a short space of time.'

Chapter Five

Jenny supposed it was only to be expected that sleep should elude her after what had happened in the garden of the restaurant, and then her realisation that she was in love with Daros. She was angry that he had upset the equilibrium of her life, and after lying awake for over an hour she rose impatiently, put on slacks and a blouse and went out into the night, to stand on the veranda looking pensively towards the mysterious expanse of the sea, whose dark, nebulous reaches were relieved only by the lights of a ship on the horizon. How lonely that ship, so small and vulnerable in a vast, awe-inspiring expanse of water that from here seemed to spread to eternity. Jenny herself felt isolated, floating in a void as fearsome as the sea.

It gave her an uneasy sensation and she was prompted to move from the veranda and seek the path beyond the fountain, leading to the little arbour she had discovered a few days ago, which she felt sure was rarely used. It was merely a rustic seat amid hibiscus bushes and oleanders with an orchid tree towering above. She sat down, savouring the quiet and the peace, but soon, becoming restless again, she rose and made her way through the villa grounds to the shore, and here her restless mood was stilled as she wandered along in her bare feet, having left her shoes by the trunk of a tree in the garden.

It was a purple velvet night with a crescent moon shining gently through the glittering brilliance of a star-laden sky and no sounds other than the primordial ones of wind and surf. It must have been like this before man came on the earth, she thought, throwing her head back and inhaling deeply. She felt totally at peace, the stars in her eyes, the wind in her hair.

She had been walking for about two or three minutes when she suddenly heard a sound; her blood froze and she stopped, fear of the unknown quivering through her. A voice came at once and she sagged with relief.

'It's only me—Daros.' Tall and masculine, he was soon beside her, towering above her as she stood there, the water just touching her toes. 'I hope I didn't scare you too much.'

'You terrified me!' she retorted. 'Do you make a practice of coming out here at this time of night?' She was angry because he had frightened her and because he had intruded into her solitude.

'As it's our private beach I do happen to have the right to be here,' he reminded her evenly. His eyes were narrowed and speculative as he added, 'What, might I ask, are *you* doing here now?'

'I wanted a walk!' Clouds masked the moon and a sudden, unexpected blackness prevented her seeing his face.

'You couldn't sleep, obviously.'

'Could you?' she countered without knowing why.

'As a matter of fact, I haven't tried. I've been busy in my study until now.'

'I see.' He began to walk on and she fell into step beside him, the warm, caressing air on her face. Magic flooded the atmosphere when presently the moon and stars emerged from the scudding grey clouds and there was light again. Jenny stole a sidelong glance at Daros and her heart caught at the sheer perfection of his classical profile.

They had reached a tiny cove within the bay where trees and undergrowth somehow found support along the rocky cliffs. Daros stopped suddenly and she almost walked into him. He caught her by the arms; the action was unnecessary and she strongly suspected that he was aware of it. Instinctively, she began to twist in order to gain her freedom, but his lean brown hands enclosed her arms and she knew a moment of exquisite fear before his mouth came down to claim her lips.

'Don't!' she protested when eventually she was free. 'Why can't you leave me alone? I'll go home if you're not careful! There's no real need for me to stay, remember.'

'I gave you the reason why you must stay. To leave here would be an insult to my father.' And on that curt reply he closed the subject and reverted to the question of her not being able to sleep. 'You're probably overtired,' he said, 'and that's why you couldn't manage to get to sleep. You've had several late nights.' He seemed a trifle anxious, she thought, and shot him a questioning glance. 'I shall have to order you to bed earlier,' he said decisively, then laughed at her outraged expression. 'You're very attractive when you're angry,' he observed, and something in his tone warned her to get out of his way as quickly as she could.

But as if anticipating her intention he shot forth a hand, catching her by the wrist before she could even make a move. He held her by the arms and stood looking down into her small, vital face, his dark eyes absorbing everything, from the high, wide forehead to the lovely eyes, filled now with a warm, unguarded tenderness of which she was unaware. Then his glance travelled to her lips and the pointed little chin that seemed, in this light, to give her an elfin look.

The silence stretched on; she was vitally aware of the romantic atmosphere—the stars and moon above and the tranquil sea caressing the golden sand at her feet, the breeze that stirred the unfolding night flowers in the undergrowth behind the shore, carrying their perfume to her nostrils. A night for romance . . . and love . . . Her heartstrings were taut, her pulses racing, her whole being alive with exquisite expectation even while a ruthless echo from her subconscious reminded her of the possibility of this dark, amorous Greek becoming her step-mother's husband. But whatever came later, this magical interlude was hers alone, this world of romance where two people, vitally aware of one another, knew that something profound and primitive was going to happen between them.

Her mind was drugged, overpowered by the sheer male magnetism of his personality that had drawn her to him, robbing her of clear thought, setting the blood drumming in her head, the nerves throughout her body on fire with longing for him. She felt the collapse of restraint as her senses reverted to the primitive and she was not only ready but eager to surren-der to his masculine attraction and dominance, to respond to his sensuous kisses and even more. . . .

His hand was inside her blouse, fingers tanta-lising, then closing in slow, sensuous motion, caressing all the time, and his dark eyes never left her face, as if he would be witness to every change of expression, every betrayal of emotion. It was a trying experience, the awareness of his visual examination, and a flush crept into her cheeks.

She quivered over and over again when his other hand slid down the full length of her spine to find her soft, pliant flesh and close upon it. With practised finesse the pressure of his hand come slowly, increasing until her body was arched against his, heat flowing through her veins like lava, white-hot, and a little moan of pleasure escaped her.

When at last he released her she leant weakly against him, sure he could feel the wild pulsating of her heart.

'What a surprising girl you are,' he said softly. 'A tempting, captivating little *koré!*' Although there seemed to be a smile in his voice Jenny thought she detected an undertone of satire and, hurt, she leant away to look into his face. It was a taut mask, unreadable. She stepped back, putting a little distance between them.

'It's late,' she murmured, instantly feeling foolish at the trite and unnecessary remark. But she was awkward, now that the passionate scene was over, because of the conviction that it had meant absolutely nothing to Daros. How many such interludes had he gone through? she wondered bleakly.

'It was already late when you came out—or perhaps I should say early.'

'Yes.' Her shrug was self-deprecating. 'It must be after one o'clock.' Her thoughts flew to Sylvia; she would be furious if she knew what was going on out here at this hour of the morning. But if she did know, perhaps she would decide to abandon everything and go home.

'What are you thinking about, Jenny?' Soft the tone, gentle the touch, as, with a hand beneath her elbow, Daros led her along the wet sand. 'Well?' He sounded attentive and eyed her with an interested expression.

'I was thinking of Sylvia,' she returned without pause, because she knew he would not tolerate prevarication.

'Your stepmother? And what were you thinking?'

'Well . . . you and she . . .'

'Yes?'

'You admitted that you might marry her.'

'And, knowing this, you allowed me to make love to you?'

'It wasn't a case of allowing,' she returned defensively. She was recovering swiftly from the feverish state and heightened emotions that had resulted from their love-making and her voice was steady and indignant. 'You would have had your way however strongly I'd protested.'

'But you didn't even attempt to protest.' His half-smile taunted. 'Nor would you protest if I did the same again.'

'I would!' Disappointment and the deep hurt of unrequited love made her angry and brought two bright spots of colour to her cheeks. 'It isn't gallant to say a thing like that!'

'Gallantry has never been one of my virtues.' His eyes were mocking. 'So you'd protest, eh?' Before she realised his intention Jenny felt his hands on her arms, tightening to inflict unnecessary pain.

'Oh!' she gasped as, with flattened palms against his chest, she used all her strength to keep their bodies apart. It was a futile effort, which was brought to an end by his taking both her hands in one of his and forcing them behind her back, where he held them firmly while he kissed her with the same dominance as before, his insistent, masterful mouth intent on forcing her lips apart. But she stubbornly managed to keep them closed. The pressure increased and tears started to her eyes.

'You brute!' she cried when, a moment later, he moved away from her, an expression of taunting amusement in his eyes. 'You—pagan!' The tears escaped, to fall unhindered down her cheeks. 'I hate you!' she flung out and would have run from him.

But, aware of her intention, he caught her by the wrist, his hold surprisingly gentle, as was his voice as he said, brushing the tears from her cheeks, 'You're too intense, child. It's all part of our modern, enlightened way of life.'

'I hate you!' she repeated, yet stood there while he found a handkerchief and handed it to her.

'You ought to take a lesson from your step-mother,' he advised, watching as she used the handkerchief on her pallid face. 'She'd teach you not to take life so seriously.' He was laughing at her but she sensed a tinge of pity too, and anger rose again, born of humiliation, for it was plain that he knew she was in love with him.

'I want to go in,' she said flatly. 'You needn't walk with me.'

'I have every intention of walking with you,' he stated firmly. Jenny made no argument but fell into step beside him. 'You're depressed,' observed Daros after a while and slowed his pace.

'No such thing. Why should I be depressed?' Her denial seemed to amuse him, for he gave a light laugh. To Jenny it sounded heartless, scraping like a rasp on her nerves.

'You're transparent too,' he asserted, 'in spite of your efforts to hide your innermost thoughts.'

'You're so clever!' was all Jenny could find to say, icy fingers gripping her heart at his quite unnecessary callousness towards her feelings for him. But she supposed he regarded her merely as another victim of his devastating charm and attraction.

'I advised you not to be so intense.' Daros stopped and when Jenny tried to go on she was caught quite firmly and forced to obey the demands of the strong fingers that gripped her wrist. Her head was tilted with an imperious gesture and she was made to look deeply into his eyes. Quivering at his touch, at the nearness of him, she could only stand there in an attitude of complete submission and wait for him to speak.

But he remained silent, looking at her, his hand beneath her chin. And when at last he bent and kissed her softly parted lips his mouth was inexpressibly gentle . . . almost tender. Tears came to her eyes; she knew he would feel them on his cheek if they should fall and valiantly held them back.

'You're so very young,' he murmured, his lips finding the soft curve of her throat and lingering there. 'So young and vulnerable.'

Something made her say, 'You don't hate me anymore, do you, Daros?'

'Hate?' He held her from him and frowned. 'Hate is a strong word, Jenny.'

'You disliked me, then.'

'Because I believed that you and your step-mother were a couple of gold-diggers.'

'And now?' she prompted breathlessly.

'I don't know,' was all he said, the shortness of his tone warning her that the matter was closed. But she knew instinctively that he was now wondering if there could be some simple explanation for those words he had heard, words that had instantly branded her a no-good in his estimation.

His hands were on her waist, spanning it, the long fingers possessive. His whole manner was domineering as he drew her to him again, his mouth seeking hers in a kiss that was as gentle as before but ardent too, so that once again Jenny found her emotions flaring, her body blending with his even without the help of the hand that was at her back, sliding along her spine, sensuously warm and tempting as the fingers curled to shape themselves to her contours. Her whole frame shook when his other hand found its way to her breast, the fingers teasing the nipple before his mouth came down to enclose the soft flesh and she knew the delight of his tongue where his fingers had been. She pressed against him with a convulsive shudder, lifting her arms to put them around his neck. She knew just what she was doing; she was fighting as only a woman in love can, willing him to discover that she had charms that could captivate, willing him to find that he cared. . . .

It was a long while later when he said, his fingers gentle as they caressed her hair, brushing it back from her wide forehead at the same

time, 'We must go in, child. It's past two o'clock.'
Yet he made no move and neither did she. He
began fastening the buttons of her blouse and
she stood as close as she could, looking at him
through her lashes. He seemed to tower above
her, masterful and superior and totally self-
possessed, which seemed a miracle after the
violence of his love-making. His hands had
roamed everywhere, his lips had caressed her
throat, her breasts, her temples. She had
thrilled to the touch of his fingers on the hyper-
sensitive places, to the rhythm of his hard body
when his ardour got out of control. This gentle
love-making had been a revelation, and it had
given Jenny hope, for it did seem that he found
something attractive about her. She could not
believe he would be so gentle and tender unless
he felt something for her, something stronger
than the physical draw.

He finished fastening the buttons but his
hands were not immediately withdrawn; she
felt the thrilling sensuousness of lean, tapered
fingers tracing the outlines of her breasts and a
smile fluttered to her lips. On what seemed an
uncontrollable impulse he kissed her full on the
lips, taking her face between his warm hands,
holding it long after he had straightened up as if
he were savouring the smooth skin against his
flesh as his fingers moved slowly over it.

At last he gave a small sigh and said, taking
one of her small hands in his, 'Come along,
Jenny. If I don't let you go now I shan't let you go
until morning.'

She coloured, then laughed, a shaky little
laugh that made him smile. But he made no

comment and it was in complete silence that they walked back along the moon-flushed beach, through the orchard and into the grounds and more formal gardens of the villa. Low and white, it shone with patrician beauty in the lambent glow of a sky brilliant with a silver luminescence created by a million stars with the moon floating in their midst.

'Good night,' he said softly when they had entered the villa and he was closing the door. 'And don't get up too early in the morning.'

'I shan't be able to,' she returned, standing for a moment in expectation of his kiss. But he seemed distant all at once, as if the scene out there had never happened. 'Daros,' she whispered, 'is—is everything all right?'

He frowned slightly, as if impatient with her question. 'Of course, Jenny. What makes you ask?' She shook her head dumbly, his hard voice having dissipated any hopes she had cherished. He had been amusing himself, nothing more.

Chapter Six

When she came into the breakfast-room at half-past nine the following morning, having slept far more restfully than she ever would have believed possible, it was to find Glavcos alone at the table, Daros and Sylvia having gone down to the pool for a swim. Feeling flat and depressed, her mind filled with uncertainty as to what she should do, Jenny was in no mood for conversation and would have forgone breakfast if Glavcos had not asked her to keep him company. She sat down and was served a few minutes later by Andros, the manservant who usually waited on them at the table in the evenings but not always at breakfast. He was there today because two of the young maids had been given the day off in order to attend a wedding in one of the tiny villages nestling in the olive-clothed foothills of the mountains.

Glavcos seemed quiet, even moody at first, and then, right out of the blue, he said, 'I suppose you have noticed what is happening between Sylvia and my son?'

Taken aback, Jenny stared, her own heartache forgotten for the moment as she returned, eyeing him curiously, 'Aren't you angry about it?'

'I was at first—in fact, I was almost crazed with jealousy. But not now. I think it will be a good thing for Daros to get married and raise a family. It's time he settled down; he's been a gay bachelor quite long enough.'

'But—' Jenny shook her head in bewilderment. 'Aren't you in love with Sylvia anymore?'

'I don't believe I ever was in love with her,' he admitted, then lapsed into contemplative silence for a while. 'There have been times recently when I've been forced to the realisation that I'm too old for marriage.'

'You didn't think that a fortnight ago,' Jenny reminded him.

'No—well, things have happened since then.'

'What things?'

In silence he looked at her across the breakfast table and instantly she knew that something of a really serious nature was troubling him.

'This is in confidence, Jenny.' He pointed a forefinger at her to emphasize his words. 'The strictest confidence, and even before I tell you what it is I want your promise that you'll not say anything either to Daros or to Sylvia.'

'I promise,' said Jenny at once.

'Well, I have had a few nasty turns lately—

within the last fortnight—the first coming two days after we'd arrived here. I seemed to have a tightening of the muscles on my left side and felt on each occasion that I might have a stroke.' He spoke with a quiver in his voice but otherwise he seemed to be quite philosophical about what might happen to him. 'That isn't all, though. The day before yesterday I woke with disturbing pains in my chest and it was the same today. I woke at five this morning and the pain was very bad, but it went away and I managed to go back to sleep.'

'You ought to see a doctor right away.' Jenny looked concernedly at him, noticing the pallor of his face. 'A thing like that shouldn't be neglected.'

'I'm not seeing a doctor yet, not until Daros is settled. I'm hoping he and Sylvia will marry, but I don't want Daros to know of my hopes yet.'

'Why not?' asked Jenny, puzzled.

'Because I believe that, initially, Daros made up to Sylvia for the sole purpose of drawing her away from me. It's the sort of thing he would do.'

'The—' Jenny found her nerves tingling; she had never even considered a possibility like that. Yet she should have, she now realised, recalling what Daros had said about protecting his father. She also recalled that certain strangeness about him, the amusement she had sensed when she coupled his name with that of her stepmother, mentioning marriage not once but several times. Jenny had wondered if he were playing with her, deriving amusement at her expense— which would have been the case if, as Glavcos believed, Daros's interest in Sylvia were a mere stratagem to draw her away from his father. What a clever move on his part! Jenny could imagine him, having achieved his object and brought about an irreparable rift between Sylvia and his father, laughing in her face as he blatantly informed her of what he had done.

But now it would seem that Glavcos was retreating voluntarily, owing to this unforeseen breakdown in his health. And he now wanted Sylvia to marry his son. . . .

'It *is* an idea," murmured Jenny, when she realised that Glavcos was awaiting her comment. But she was forced to add, 'It can't be accepted as a certainty, though.'

'I am convinced of it,' he said without reservation. 'Daros has always hated the idea of my remarrying. He adored his mother, but that's not altogether the reason for his objection. He's convinced that any woman I become friendly with is after my money, and I admit—' He stopped and a rueful grin took years from his age. 'I admit that I've been fond of the women— although I haven't courted one as young as your stepmother, hence the shock Daros had when he saw her.'

Glavcos's expression changed and he became reflective. 'I know that money would never enter dear Sylvia's head, so Daros was all wrong when he judged her, as I've told him many times. She has never struck me as mercenary. All she wants is someone to care for her and protect her because, as you must have realised, she's the fragile, helpless type who needs someone strong to depend on.' He continued for some moments to praise Sylvia's virtues, reverting now and then to the fact that she needed protecting. Jenny listened patiently, trying to appear interested but fearing very much that a dry expression had settled on her face.

'As I was saying,' continued Glavcos, 'I don't want Daros to know of my wishes regarding him and Sylvia, simply because I feel that if he should discover, at this stage, that I have no intention of marrying Sylvia he's likely to give her up and send you both home. What I'm hoping for is that, given enough time, he'll become so enamoured of her beauty and other rather special gifts that he'll find he can't live without her.' He paused a moment and Jenny saw by the sudden twinkle in his eye that he had become diverted again. 'The activities of a bridegroom are not exactly the best for a man whose heart might give out at any minute, so you'll agree that I'm being wise in my decision not to marry her.'

Jenny coloured and he laughed, which only served to increase her embarrassment. 'Don't say your heart is going to give out,' she protested, having managed to regain her composure. 'Won't you see a doctor right away? After all, your health's far more important than your son's marriage to Sylvia.' If only she could persuade him to drop this idea of holding off in order to give Daros time to become captivated by Sylvia's glamour and sex appeal. It was galling to Jenny because she now felt that if Daros were given the information that his father had abandoned the idea of marrying Sylvia it might just come to pass that he would finish with her. But, given time, there was no knowing what would happen; he might even fall in love with her.

It occurred to Jenny that even if Daros did give Sylvia up he would never look at *her*, so why should she adopt this dog-in-the-manger attitude? If I were a nice girl, Jenny said to herself, I'd be delighted at the idea of Sylvia's getting what she wants—marriage to a wealthy man.

'I've said I'm not seeing a doctor and I mean it.' Glavcos spoke at last, answering her question. He was buttering toast and Jenny could not help but notice the enlarged knuckle bones, pearly-white beneath the parchment skin, and the veins standing out, blue-black and knotted. Naturally her thoughts swung to Sylvia, whose hands, with their long, tapered fingers, were beautiful.

'Tell me,' Glavcos said, 'did you really want me to marry your stepmother?'

'I—er—well—'

'You needn't be afraid of offending me,' he interrupted in a quiet voice. 'It was only to be expected that you'd not want her to throw herself away on an old man like me.' A serious expression settled on his face. Jenny marvelled at his mood; he seemed to have grown up at last. 'But I don't think you can have any objection to her marrying Daros,' he went on, picking up a piece of toast and holding it close to his mouth. 'They're of an age and they're both very attractive people. I'm sure you'll agree that a more suitable match could never be made for either of them and that you'd be as happy as I would if they were to marry.'

Jenny bit her lip till it hurt. She wondered what this old man would say were she to tell him that, far from being happy, she would be the most *un*happy person on the entire island because she herself was in love with his son.

'I d-don't know what to say,' she murmured. 'Perhaps you are—are mistaken—I mean.' She looked at him. 'Are you hoping for Daros to fall in love with Sylvia?'

'Few Greek men fall in love,' admitted Glavcos matter-of-factly. 'But Sylvia has all it takes to make a man happy.'

Jenny found herself nodding in agreement, her thoughts reverting to Daros's own belief that love was not important, not one of the prerequisites to marriage, whereas physical attraction was.

She was still brooding over what Glavcos had said when, a couple of hours later, she decided to go down to the sea for a swim. Sylvia was on the lawn, cool and lovely as ever, the long lashes fringing her blue eyes sending delectable shadows onto her cheeks.

'I'm going for a swim in the sea.' Jenny's voice was flat, discouraged. 'Do you want to come?'

'Not at this moment, darling. I've had a lovely swim in the pool with Daros. Oh, but doesn't he look magnificent with nothing on!'

'Nothing!' exclaimed Jenny, staring in disbelief.

'Well, *practically* nothing.' Sylvia laughed.

'How shocked you looked! You're only a child, really—'

'I'm not!' denied Jenny fiercely. 'I wish you'd stop treating me like one!'

'Oh, all right,' mildly, but with a faint catch in her voice. 'How prickly you are these days, Jenny. Can it be that you're jealous of my conquest of the handsome Daros?'

Jenny felt a dryness affecting her tongue. 'Why should I care about you and Daros?' she demanded, trying to sound casual.

'I've an idea you'd like him for yourself.' Languidly Sylvia moved the hand that had been idling on the edge of the lounger and sought for the gold cigarette case lying on the velvet-smooth grass below. 'You said it was just a bit of fun you two were having, but you'd never convince me that you've found it possible to resist his superlative charm.'

'I suppose,' Jenny snapped back, 'that you think he's in love with you.'

'Think?' The shapely eyebrows lifted. 'I *know* he's in love with me.'

'How do you know?'

'He told me so.'

'He did?' Jenny knew she was lying, but allowed it to pass without comment. 'What about Glavcos?' she asked, eyeing Sylvia curiously.

'I don't believe he wants to marry me—oh, I know it's not very flattering to be forced to a conclusion like that. But the very fact that he's not jealous, that he's never protested when Daros has given me his attention, convinces me that he's changed his mind.' Sylvia lapsed into silence, a frown puckering her brow. She inhaled, deeply, then allowed the smoke to escape through lips that had formed into a pout. 'How fickle men are,' she complained. 'Who'd have thought that Glavcos would prove to be so inconstant? I must admit I am exceedingly disappointed in him.'

In spite of the heaviness within her, Jenny had to smile. 'You're the limit, Sylvia!'

'You mean it's unreasonable of me to be hurt by what Glavcos has done?' The baby-blue eyes registered indignation. 'I wish I could understand you, Jenny.'

'I'm going for my swim,' Jenny said decisively. 'This conversation's becoming absurd.'

'You look very sexy in that outfit,' observed Sylvia, as her stepdaughter turned to go. 'I don't know if I did right in letting you buy it.' Her voice reminisced. 'I saw it first, if you remember.'

'I remember,' she said, with a sigh of impatience. 'You said it wasn't brief enough for you—the bikini, I mean, not the wrap.'

'All the same, I feel sure that dear Daros would love to see me in it. If you don't mind, Jenny love, I'll borrow it tomorrow.'

'Borrow it if you want,' was all Jenny replied before she turned and walked away in the direction of the *perivoli* that separated the villa grounds proper from the palm-fringed area that backed up to the pale golden beach. In this orchard were olives, tangerines and lemons, apples and luscious figs. How wonderful to grow one's own fruits, she mused, as she treaded her way through the long grass growing beneath the trees. She was trying hard to keep her mind off what was taking place, not to recall anything said either by Glavcos or by Sylvia regarding Daros. But more than anything else, she was making a desperate effort to forget what had happened between herself and Daros last night.

But it was not to be expected that she would succeed in putting any of it out of her mind, and although she enjoyed the swim in water that was pleasantly warm and smooth as silk, her mind brooded the whole time. What complications! Glavcos no longer wanting to marry Sylvia, and Sylvia no longer interested in Glavcos but hoping to marry his son instead, then the totally unforeseen mischance of Jenny herself falling in love with Daros. On top of all this was Daros's own attitude, towards both Jenny and her stepmother. By his own admission, Sylvia was gifted with certain attractions that appealed to him, and he had not hesitated to own that marriage to Sylvia was possible. Yet at the same time he could, on every occasion that happened to present itself, make love to Jenny.

Where was the sense of any of it? she wondered, her thoughts so confused that she came out of the water, deciding to go back to the villa and try to relax her mind by reading the book she had started yesterday.

After reaching the shore, she had just picked up the towel when she saw Daros swinging along, clad only in swimming trunks and dangling a multi-coloured towel at his side. He came to her, tall and lithe and very brown.

Embarrassment flooded over her at the memory of their last meeting, but somehow she managed to hide it, much to her own surprise. She regarded him coolly, returning his quiet 'Good morning,' and it was only when he said he was glad that she had obeyed his order and stayed in bed that she betrayed any kind of emotion.

'I stayed in bed,' she returned tartly, 'because it suited me to do so, not in response to the *advice* you proffered!'

Daros laughed at the emphasis on the word 'advice', and Jenny caught her breath, as she always did, at the sheer attractiveness of him. And try as she would she found it impossible not to let her eyes roam over his tall, perfectly proportioned figure, which at once gave the impression of power and strength despite its slender, almost boyish lines. She looked up at him and there was an impenetrable air about him that seemed to add to his distinction, as did the impression of arrogance and superiority, which, although making her feel small and insignificant, also made her profoundly aware of her own femininity.

'You've had your swim,' he said, watching as she began to towel herself down. 'But aren't you going in again?'

'No, I don't think so.' Her mind was a tangle of uncertainty, the instinct to leave him and go back to the villa fighting against the desire to stay. 'I was intending to read.'

He made no move but remained with his eyes focused on her, watching the play of emotion in her expressive grey eyes. 'Come in with me.' It was a command, though spoken softly. 'The water's always pleasantly warm at this time of year.'

Did he really want her company? It would seem so, she thought, dropping her towel on the sand. 'All right, I'll come in with you.'

They swam side by side in the calm cerulean sea with the velvet Aegean sky above, clear and blue except for a few curdles of fair-weather cumulus, smooth-based and high, tinted golden by the sun. It was an idyllic morning, with the only sign of life—apart from themselves—being a couple of sea-birds perched on a rock at the far end of the bay, their motionless forms silhouetted against the sky.

'It's wonderful!' she exclaimed, all her previous misery and despair miraculously washed away, and she was in a dream-world of happiness, her heart light and beating just a little more quickly than was normal. 'How lovely the water is!'

When eventually they came out Daros stood for a long moment, his dark eyes subjecting her to a prolonged and intense scrutiny. The Greek sun had given her face a tan of honey-gold brushed with peach to accentuate the high, delicately formed cheek bones. Her limpid grey eyes, thickly fringed, stared unblinkingly into his, while a hand lifted rather unsteadily to flick her wet hair from her forehead. A smile fluttered, resulting more from her feeling of awkwardness than anything else, but to Daros it was both a challenge and an invitation.

'You look beguilingly youthful and innocent,' was his surprising comment, and before she could even suspect his intention he had bent his dark head and kissed her full on the lips. 'No protests?'

She made no answer because her lids had become heavy and she knew it would not take much to make her cry, for, as far as Daros was concerned, last night might never have happened.

His eyes moved to her figure, the wet costume clinging seductively to the tender curves, and, confused, she took up the towel and spread it out as a cover. The dark eyes laughed and crinkles fanned attractively from the corners. Jenny swallowed, one half of her mind wishing she had never met this man while the other, even now, thrilled to his nearness, to the fact that, whatever his motive for the attention he was giving her, at least she had it, for there was no doubt at all that he was content to be with her.

'I never asked if you had a boy-friend at home.' He was spreading his towel; she stood irresolute. Her towel was taken from her and put very close to his. 'Sit down,' he invited. 'We'll soon dry off in this heat.' She obeyed, relieved to find her awkwardness dissolving.

'I haven't a boy-friend,' she answered belatedly.

'I wonder why.' He was sitting on the towel, his long legs stretched out, his arms behind him to support his body. 'You're attractive enough to be in great demand.'

She coloured daintily at the compliment . . . and noticed a fleeting change of expression that she would very much have liked to understand.

'Perhaps,' she reflected, her thoughts on David Bransley, 'I've been too choosey.'

'Could be.' He leant further back on the support of his arms and his body seemed longer
than ever. 'Was money the problem?'

'Money?' she repeated, puzzled.

'You wanted to marry wealth?'

Her teeth gritted and her eyes flashed fire.
'Must you always insult me?'

'Jenny,' he said with some asperity, 'you're
becoming tiresomely touchy. Why don't you
answer my question?'

'Because it ought never to have been asked!'
She looked away to where the summits of the
gaunt mountains cut raggedly into the sky. The
whole of the centre of the island was mountain-
ous, a volcanic mass formed aeons ago, before
man came on the earth.

The silence continued and at last she was
driven to break it, saying coldly, 'I don't expect
you to be anything but sceptical when I say I
turned down an offer of marriage from a man
who was exceedingly wealthy.' She stared directly at him, half challenging, half defiant. She
looked very young and faintly rebellious, and a
quizzical smile tugged at the corners of Daros's
mouth.

'You jump to conclusions far too easily,' he
said, and some strange inflection in his tone
made her ask, 'I was wrong, then? You do
believe me?'

He nodded without hesitation, and her spirits
lifted.

'What made you turn him down?'

'I didn't love him,' she replied simply.

'Is love so important to you?' His voice had a

curious ring again and his glance was withdrawn. Where was all this leading, Jenny wondered, and where was the mocking derision he had shown when, only last night, she had talked about love? Jenny felt there were depths to his character that were scarcely ever revealed.

'To most women love is important.' She had no notion of the catch in her voice or of the wistful shadows in her eyes. 'I can't imagine marriage without love.' She lifted her face, aware of the pain in her heart but not of the plea in her eyes, so she wondered at his changing expression and at the uncontrolled pulsation of a nerve in the hollow of his throat.

'Come,' he said abruptly, the change in him dramatic. 'It's time we were moving.'

His strides were long and brisk as they walked back to the villa; he appeared to be angry with himself and her spirits flagged again. What an unpredictable man! She could not conceive what had happened to make him change so suddenly. If the idea had not been too absurd she could have believed he was emotionally affected by her assertion that she could not imagine marriage without love.

One thing had certainly taken root in her mind: Daros did not now think nearly so badly of her as he had at first.

As they entered the grounds of the villa they saw Sylvia on the flower-draped patio, a vivid scarlet bougainvillaea vine forming the perfect foil for her pale, fragile beauty. Did Daros catch his breath? Jenny slanted him a swift sideways glance but learnt nothing from the mask of his face. She knew instinctively, though, that his mood had undergone another change and he was no longer angry.

'So there you are!' Sylvia's husky, low-toned voice was pettish. 'Er—have you been swimming?' The blue eyes were brilliant with anger as they settled on her stepdaughter's face.

'I should have thought it was obvious that we'd been swimming,' answered Daros on a satirical note. 'You, apparently, have been reading.' His eyes wandered to the open book on the marble-topped table at which Sylvia was sitting, her slender curves daringly revealed as all she had on was a bikini of so brief a design as to be practically useless. Jenny, watching Daros's face, still read nothing, but with a dejected little sigh she felt sure he must be moved by Sylvia's beauty.

'I've been trying to read but wasn't very successful. It's been lonely sitting here, all on my own.' At the familiar catch in her voice Jenny's lips tightened. How well she did it! Sylvia fluttered Daros a glance from under her lashes. 'I'd no idea you wanted another swim,' she murmured huskily, 'or I'd have suggested coming with you.'

Daros's smile was devastating. It was the unmistakable smile of a man affected by a woman's charm and beauty, and his voice was almost a caress when, after a small, unfathomable silence, he spoke. 'I thought you wanted to rest for a while.'

'You'd have gone with Daros?' interposed Jenny, lifting her eyebrows significantly. 'But if you wanted a swim you could have come with me. I did ask you,' she said, determined not to let her get away with anything. 'You said you preferred to relax, since you'd had one swim already. . . .' Jenny's voice trailed into silence as, catching Daros's expression, she felt sure he was suppressing mirth.

'So you've been bored.' Daros spoke into the silence, adding after the merest hesitation, 'Well, how about my taking you for a drive in the car and then to lunch at a *taverna* up in the mountains?' The charm of his smile brought an instant response.

'Oh, how pleasant that sounds, Daros! Yes, I'd love to go driving with you!' A covert glance in her stepdaughter's direction, an almost imperceptible light of triumph, before she said in dulcet tones, 'You'll keep dear Glavcos company, won't you, Jenny, dear? It wouldn't be very nice for him to take his lunch alone.'

'I might go out myself,' gritted Jenny.

'Out?' This came sharply from Daros. 'Where would you go?'

'There are several very good *cafeneions* in the village that I've been hoping to try. It'll be interesting to see what they serve in the way of Greek food.' She had no intention of leaving Glavcos to eat alone at lunch-time, but anger made her add, a hint of defiance and challenge in her eyes as she glanced at Daros, 'I might see Helios. I'm sure he will be very happy to have lunch with me.'

A dark look accompanied the tightening of Daros's jaw. 'I believe,' he said tautly, 'that I told you not to become familiar with that young man. He has a reputation as a womaniser.'

115

'But is he any different from most other Greek men?'

'I'm not talking about comparisons,' he snapped. 'You will have your lunch here, with my father, understand?'

'Daros!' exclaimed Sylvia, assuming a shocked expression. 'You can't dictate to dear Jenny like that! She ought to be free to cultivate this young man if she wishes . . . and I am sure that, secretly, she likes him a lot—'

'How can it be a secret if you know about it?' countered Jenny, for the first time in her life feeling she could hit somebody. 'Anyway, this thing about Helios is my own business! If I have the chance to lunch with him, then I shall certainly do just that!' And before either of them could speak she was out of hearing, having run from the patio into the villa, entering through an open French window.

Chapter Seven

Contrary to her expectations, Jenny was destined to go out for her lunch after all, Glavcos having been invited to join two friends for lunch at the Astir Beach Hotel.

'They're here, on Camina, from a cruise ship that's staying for nine hours,' he added, after telling Jenny he was going out. 'They live in Athens and have taken this cruise to the islands. One of them phoned me and invited me to join them.' He was obviously happy at the idea of going out but there was a tinge of anxiety in his voice as he said, 'You'll be all right on your own? You'll not feel lonely?'

'Of course not." She smiled. 'But you—take care, won't you?"

'You're a nice little girl to worry about me,' he said and left her, going to his room to change.

Little girl . . . Sylvia thought of her as a child, and Daros had described her as very young and vulnerable. She went to her bedroom to stare critically at her reflection in the long, gilt-framed mirror. Yes, she was forced to admit that she looked younger than her age, but as there was nothing to be done about it she put it from her mind. And at the same time she decided she would not lunch at home but would go into the village and sample some Greek food.

The *cafeneion* that she chose was right on the beach, an outdoor café overhung with vines for shade and set in a garden where pink and white and red oleanders were in full bloom, these latter forming a magnificent and decorative hedge along two sides of the large plot on which the *cafeneion* was situated. Butterflies hovered over the bright vermillion blossoms of the pomegranate trees smouldering in one corner and then flitted to the pretty yellow flowers of the prickly pear close by. Soft and mournful *bouzouki* music drifted over the sunlit garden from inside the low white building, and stocky men in dark blue jackets moved about among the tables, flashing smiles in her direction. At one table two men sat playing *tavla* and drinking *ouzo* while several more stood over them and watched, worry beads clicking and twirling in their strong brown hands. On the sea, several brightly coloured *caïques* bobbed about while on a large pavement at one side of the jetty a man was slapping a newly caught octopus, creating the frothy white lather that was essential to make the flesh tender.

Having been shown to a table for two, Jenny sat back in her chair, and although her pensive gaze wandered to the silver ribbon of road snaking up the mountain to the restaurant where Sylvia and Daros would be dining, she was able to enjoy her surroundings, to appreciate the typically Greek setting, the atmosphere that brought forcibly to her consciousness the fact that she was in the East, for there was a marked absence of women. Perfumes from the flowers mingled with the salt-tangy smell of the sea, then across it all drifted the appetising odour of kebabs cooking over a charcoal grill. A menu was handed to her; she had just begun to study it when she felt a tap on her shoulder and, turning, looked up into the smiling face of Helios. What a coincidence, was her first thought, while instantly on this came the stern, forbidding voice of Daros telling her she was not to become familiar with Helios and that she was to have her lunch at home with his father. Well, his father was not at home.

'Yassoo!' greeted Helios and he sat down on the vacant chair without asking her leave. 'Why are you here all alone?'

She explained that everyone had gone out and said she thought it would be a good opportunity to try one of the restaurants in the village. 'I chose this one merely by chance,' she added finally.

'You choose the best one. I come here always. I work at the bank in the main street so it is a walk but—how do you say?—worth it.' He seemed to take it for granted that she would want his company and he casually reached over to pick up a menu from the next table, which was vacant. 'What are you eating?'

'Can you recommend anything?' Jenny gave a wry grimace. 'I'm ashamed to admit it, but I haven't had much Greek food at all.'

'They do not serve it at the Villa Camina?'

'I rather think they changed the menus to suit my stepmother and me. The food's the same as we have at home, mostly.'

'Well,' he mused, turning his attention to the menu in his hand. 'Let me see . . . I like *dolmades* for a starter—stuffed vine leaves—delicious! Then the *barbouni*'s very good; it's fish, red mullet you call it, and cooked with herbs over a charcoal grill. It comes with green salad and our fried potatoes.'

Already Jenny's mouth was watering; she agreed at once to have what he had recommended. She was determined to enjoy her lunch, to forget all about Daros and Sylvia, lunching up there in the forested hills. She had the pleasant company of Helios; he was a good-looking, amiable young man and she had been fortunate in meeting him here since she had not really relished sitting on her own, the object of stares from every man present. As they ate their *dolmades* she asked Helios about this staring and he laughed and glanced around.

'Greek men think a lot about sex—but surely you already have discovered this?' Jenny coloured delicately but made no answer. 'We like to look at a woman's body, to admire her figure and her legs.'

'And what about her face?' Jenny was impelled to say and again he laughed.

'Important, true,' he admitted, 'but the figure . . .' His voice trailed into silence and Jenny turned swiftly. Two bright young things had come strolling up from the beach, clad in shorts and carrying shoulder bags and cameras. From the cruise ship, guessed Jenny, turning back to her food. 'See what I mean?' Helios was grinning, showing strong white teeth. 'We can't help ourselves.'

'It's crazy!' declared Jenny. 'There are so many other interesting things in life.'

'But to a Greek, none as interesting as the delightful form of a woman.'

She gave up and in fact had to laugh. Helios's buoyancy was infectious and she was not long in catching it, with the result that they laughed a lot during the meal. And they drank a heady red wine into the bargain, which certainly had something to do with the way Jenny felt when at length they rose from the table. Helios insisted on paying and she stood on her own while he went inside the café to pay at the desk. A few bronzed bodies could be seen spread out on the golden sand, and a few people were in the sea. A lull in the chatter around her coincided with a pause in the *bouzouki* music, allowing the whirring of cicadas to invade the silence.

Jenny gave a contented sigh as she watched Helios approaching, nodding and smiling to acquaintances as he made his way towards her. He was handsome in a very different way from Daros, she mused. More heavily built, so his face was fuller; not so tall, so he seemed a little overweight—in fact, she was sure he was, but that did not detract from the impression of muscled strength and Jenny found herself thinking that it would not be a good thing for anyone to pick a quarrel with him. Why such a thought should cross her mind she could not have said, but she felt instinctively that, like Daros, he was a man who would want—and get—all his own way.

'I'm off for the afternoon,' he said as he reached her. 'How about coming for a drive with me?'

'You're off?' She looked at him with a puzzled expression. 'You didn't mention it before.'

'No; I was thinking to go home and garden for my father. But I'd like much better to show you my country.'

Jenny put a hand to her head, wishing she had not been persuaded to have that last glass of wine. 'I think I had better go back to the villa.' She had walked down but she said she would be grateful for a lift if he would give her one.

'I think the drive in the fresh air will do good to you, Jenny,' he said, and because her eyes had strayed to the mountain again she suddenly felt inexpressibly flat and depressed, with the result that she found herself saying, 'Yes, perhaps a drive will do me good. Where shall we go?'

'Let's just drive at first, then we'll go to the Sanctuary of Apollo on the other side of the mountain. You like antiquities, yes? So you are sure to enjoy walking in the ruins.' His voice held amusement; his brown eyes had a merry twinkle in their depths. Jenny's shoulders lifted as if a weight had been taken from them. It was impossible to be downcast when in the company of someone as carefree and effervescent as Helios, and she was remembering that in Greek mythology he was the God of Light, of the sun itself.

'I didn't know there was a Sanctuary of Apollo here,' she was saying as they walked to where his car was parked, beneath the shade of a carob tree.

'There are Sanctuaries of Apollo in many places in Greece.' He seemed faintly surprised at her lack of knowledge. 'Our Greek myths are most fascinating a subject; you should read about them.'

'I will once I get back home.'

'You're going home?' He was holding the car door while she entered and she did not know if his lips touched her hair or whether she imagined it. The fact was that her head was not at all as clear as she would have wished.

'I must go home. I have a house—well, it partly belongs to my stepmother,' she amended. 'It's standing empty and I'm not happy about it. I'm beginning to think of burglars.' It was not the thought of burglars that worried her and made her eager to get back; it was the knowledge that her hurts would begin to heal only after she had left the Villa Camina.

'I'm sorry you must go. Will it be soon?' Helios was behind the wheel. Jenny looked at his hands and compared them with the strong brown hands that had caressed her so gently, as if their owner really cared.

'I hope it will be soon,' she replied, leaning

back against the upholstery with the intention of enjoying the drive. The windows were open, letting in a cool breeze as the car bowled along the waterfront before turning into the olive-clothed hills.

'Is your stepmother a friend to Mr. Daros?'

'Of course,' briefly and with a touch of asperity designed to daunt him in case he should think of pursuing the subject. But she had reckoned without his curiosity and determination.

'Then it's a wonder, because it is well known to all on this island that Mr. Daros has never liked any woman his father has been friendly with.' Jenny said nothing, but her silence, though pointed, was no more effective than her unaccommodating tone had been a moment earlier. 'Mr. Glavcos is old now; everybody thinks he is too old to marry. Your stepmother looks so young. And she is certainly very beautiful. People talk, you know.'

'She's been the object of gossip?' Jenny knew her stepmother would hate that.

'Well, of course. On so small an island like this everybody knows everything about their neighbours. And the Kyrou family are the richest and most—how do you say it?—respected family so of course we are all wanting to know what they are doing. What age is your stepmother?'

'I'm not telling you, Helios. She would not want me to divulge her age.'

'You said she was young, I remember.'

'Comparatively young.'

'Many years younger than Mr. Glavcos. I think that Mr. Daros will stop it,' he declared. 'Shall you be sorry?'

'Helios,' said Jenny, in a voice of chill finality, 'I am not intending to discuss my stepmother so we shall change the subject, if you don't mind.'

'Are you angry with me?' he inquired, and she thought that even if she were her anger would not last long, for there were both apology and laughter in her companion's voice, and in his eyes was a twinkle it was difficult to resist.

She had to laugh as she answered, 'I don't believe you'd care very much if I was!'

'I would be heartbroken!'

'Fibber!'

'Fibber?' He turned his dark head, taking his eyes completely off the road. 'What is this word? I have never heard of it.'

She paused a moment. To say it meant liar was unthinkable. 'Never mind, Helios. It's too difficult to explain.'

He accepted that and they drove on in silence for a while, Jenny's whole attention on the view she was seeing from her window, changing vistas and changing colours, with now and then a burst of crimson from poinsettias or hibiscus, or the red cupolas and white campaniles to denote a village nestling in the hills. Several times Helios slowed down for sheep on the road or women in black, shepherding tinkling goats, bringing them from the pastures. As they passed through a village of low white villas, bright with flowers in tubs and pots, she was confronted with the familiar sight of men sprawled at the tables of an outdoor café, playing cards, smoking, and twirling worry beads. Worry in Greece must be a man's function, she thought wryly.

The women had no time. At another café a man was cooking *souvlaki* on a charcoal grill over which hung a pall of black smoke, and from which came the delicious smell of herbs and sizzling meat.

Helios eventually drove through a pass in the foothills of the mountains and into Jenny's view came a cluster of tall columns among slender cypresses and chestnut trees. The Sanctuary of Apollo, she surmised.

'It looks fascinating!' she exclaimed, eager to reach the site. 'Will there be many people there?'

Helios shook his head. 'It's not been, uh, commercialised; you won't be hearing here guides babbling at you, saying always the same thing over and over.'

'Guides are useful,' protested Jenny in support of them. 'I like to know the history of what I'm seeing.'

'I can explain all of it to you. I think anyway we shall have the place alone because although there is a cruise ship in, the passengers all will want to be at the shopping and cafés.'

The Sanctuary lay on a plateau and as they drew closer to the ruins Jenny noticed how weathered and mellowed the columns were, rising tall and straight against the magical blue of the Grecian sky.

Helios slowed as he negotiated the last few bends in the narrow road, then he stopped to see where he would park the car. 'I will put it there, in the shade,' he decided, turning to give her a smile. 'You enjoyed the drive, yes?'

'It was terrific.'

'I like you, Jenny, because you appreciate things you see. Many people never see what is around them.' He parked and they got out. He took her arm as they strolled over to where the Temple of Apollo stood, the base of the columns covered with wild vegetation, the most attractive being the fragile poppies, nodding in the breeze.

As Helios had predicted, they had the sacred precincts to themselves—no tourists to chatter and snap cameras, nothing to disturb the peace or mar the virgin beauty that nature had created all around the holy place where in ancient times men came to worship the son of Zeus and Leto, the god of all that was good and pure in life. Jenny felt it must have been wonderful to believe in the pagan gods no matter what people today thought about it.

'It's such a pity that time has been so destructive,' she said with a sad inflection. 'Just look at all the columns that have fallen down and been broken.'

'Earth movements,' said Helios. 'These are happening all the time but most people don't know about them.' He paused and smiled at her. 'It is a very ancient site, remember, and much can happen in so many thousand years.'

'It's that old?' Her eyes widened. 'It seems incredible that anything at all is left, then.' Helios said nothing; he was still holding her arm, and she felt his body touching hers as they walked along. She did not particularly like the contact but when she moved away he moved as well.

'Have you ever been to Delphi, or to the island of Delos?' he asked.

'No, this is the only Greek island I've visited, and I haven't been on the mainland at all.'

'Pity. There are wonderful Sanctuaries to Apollo in those places. You must stay for a while,' he added decisively. 'Why do you want to go home?'

'I've told you—I have a house.'

He merely shrugged and they walked on past more ruins and steps and columns gleaming in mellow loneliness against the fierce metallic rays of the afternoon sun, past more tall cypresses and pines restless in the breeze, and then, just over a rise, came the breathtaking panorama of the sea, rolling away in a wine-dark expanse of velvet smoothness towards the line where a haze of gold and mauve hung over the horizon.

'It's . . . beautiful,' breathed Jenny, wondering how one found words to describe such a scene. For a long while she stood there, conscious of Helios close to her, and then suddenly, with a flash of imagination, she saw Daros beside her, here in this lonely, magical place that did not seem to be part of a real world at all, but something so pure and primitive that it existed before time began. She lifted her face and pensive gaze to the man beside her . . . and all she saw was a leaner face, darker and more severe, but noble and arrogant. Her heart felt as if a sword had managed somehow to pierce it and the pain was excruciating, for all she saw now was the picture of Daros and Sylvia together, perhaps in some place like this, for it was likely that he would take a long time in getting home, stopping on the way to admire the view.

'What do you think about, Jenny?' Helios's arm came about her waist as he asked the question; she noticed a hoarse inflection in his voice and frowned.

'Nothing that would interest you,' she answered, trying to draw away, but his arm tightened.

'You would like to make harmony?'

'Make harmony?' She tried again to draw away, inserting her fingers beneath his hand to loosen his grip on her waist. 'What do you mean?'

'In Greece we have a saying that we make harmony if we want to be very good friends.'

She looked around, her heart beginning to beat erratically as she admitted to her foolishness in coming up here with a man she scarcely knew, a man whom Daros had described as a womaniser. His face was close to hers now as he repeated his question, then added that this was a very romantic place to make harmony.

'I have no intention of making harmony, as you call it, so you needn't keep on asking me.' She was terribly afraid, aware that the colour had left her face. 'I want to go back—it's later than I thought,' she added with a glance at her wristwatch. 'How long will it take to drive back to the village?'

No expression on his face, but his mouth seemed to have compressed a little. 'We shall not go back yet, Jenny. I want to make harmony with you.' She felt his arm slide further round her waist and she twisted to get away. He laughed. 'You're not shy. You're only pretending! I have had girls before who pretend they are shy or scared, but it's only a little game they play to make it more exciting.'

'It is *not* a game!' she cried, managing to drag herself from his hold. 'I have no intention of making harmony, so you can forget it! I'm going home!' She turned and began to run towards the car, desperately hoping he would take her refusal seriously and drive her back to the village. He followed, but grasped her wrist and swung her right around with a jerk that brought her up against his chest. Frantically, she pushed her hands between her body and his, bringing them hard against him, but her strength was no match for his. She glanced round wildly, a stab of sheer terror the prelude to a conviction that if she came out of this situation unscathed she would be exceedingly fortunate. There was not a sign of life anywhere other than a few tethered goats on the plain of olives that swept right down to the sea. 'Let me go! You dare not molest me—I am a guest of Mr. Kyrou—'

'He will never know that we have made love. You won't tell him or anyone else.' He was bending her body over backwards, his hand caressing her waist and moving upwards. She saw his dark face above her and as her terror increased it became a misted blur, with his features scarcely recognisable; she must be going to faint, she thought, and in desperation began to struggle furiously, fear and anger and hatred mingling to give her strength. And, somehow, she did derive sufficient force to thrust him off, and she wondered just how long the respite would be as she watched him go staggering backwards, arms flailing the air as he tried to regain his balance. But he failed and Jenny's eyes dilated as she saw him step onto a fallen column and crash to the ground, one leg buckled beneath him, a cry that was something between an oath and a strangled wail of pain rending the silence. She could only stare, a hand stealing to her throat, every nerve in her body darting about, out of control. What had she done? He was so still. With a tremendous effort she went to him, and to her utter relief he opened his eyes to glower at her, his mouth twisting—whether with pain or fury she could not tell.

'Are you hurt—?' What a stupid question, she thought. But her mind was still hazy from the wine, and now this. . . . 'What are we to do?'

'I've broken my leg.' He groaned and put his head in his hands. 'You did it!'

'You had no right to molest me!' she retorted, stung that he should blame her for what had happened. 'What did you expect me to do but try to defend myself?'

'Can you drive my car?' he asked, lifting his face again.

'I—well, I did drive at home.'

'Then don't stand there! Get in it and bring some help to me!'

Her eyes glinted. Sorry as she was for him, she was furiously resentful of the attitude he was taking. 'I've a good mind to leave you here,' she threatened, but of course she did not mean it. However, her words seemed to have a sobering effect on him and when he spoke again it was in a much more conciliatory tone of voice.

'If you will drive down to the village and get me an ambulance—'

'It would simplify matters if you could manage to get to the car,' she suggested. 'I could then take you straight to the hospital.' He did not answer immediately and she added, her eyes roving his crumpled form, 'Are you sure your leg's broken?'

'Didn't you hear the crack?'

'No—I suppose I was thinking of—of myself.' And the fact that by some miracle she had managed to thrust him away. He was edging his body into a sideways position, and Jenny's eyes were questioning until he withdrew a small bunch of keys. 'Don't be long,' he begged. 'I'm in terrible pain.' He held out the keys; she took them from him, stood for a few seconds, her heart still pounding wildly against her ribs, then turned and without a backward glance made her way to where he had left his car.

The car was large, the road perilously narrow in places, so progress was slow, and it gave Jenny more time to think. How long would it take to drive to the hospital? She had no intention of going back to the site; once she had ordered the ambulance she could go home, but it would still be so late that Daros would demand to know where she had been. Yet what real right did he have to ask? She could refuse to say where she had been, and what could he do about it? He might try to convince himself that, as she was a guest in his home, he had certain rights over her—he had in fact said that already—but that did not mean that Jenny had to accept his authority. Let him ask! Let him even try to

132

browbeat her! She would stand fast and not tell either him or Sylvia where she had been and what had happened. It was her secret and it would stay that way.

But she had reckoned without the intervention of fate. Having reached the village, she suddenly realised that it would be simpler, and would save time, if she stopped at the first shop she came to and asked if she could use the telephone. That the shop happened to be a men's outfitters she already knew since she had been into the village several times, both on her own and with Sylvia. That there was one single customer in the dimly lit interior she knew the moment she entered, but in her haste she merely looked at the proprietor and said urgently, 'There's been an accident and I need to use a telephone. If you would let me use yours—?'

'Jenny!' She swung round on hearing her name, and every vestige of colour left her face. 'An accident?' Daros seemed anxious, she thought, as his eyes roamed over her from head to foot. 'What—?'

'You!' was all she could find to say, the one word spoken in choking accents.

'You want to use the phone, you said,' intervened the proprietor. He was obviously curious to know what was going on. 'Of course you can use it.'

'What's happened?' demanded Daros, his eyes wide open and inquiring. 'Obviously it isn't you who's been in an accident.'

'It's—it's . . .' Her voice trailed away to silence. What price now her determination to stand up to Daros? She was trembling all over under his scrutiny and furious with herself because of it. Why couldn't she be stronger, and belligerent, ready to give as much as she got?

'Well?' prompted Daros gently. 'You came in here as though it were urgent.'

'We—I need an ambulance,' she managed at last, thinking of Helios up there, miles from anywhere, in pain, and in the intense heat as well. 'It's to—to go up to the Sanctuary—'

'Sanctuary?' interrupted Daros. 'And who's up there?'

'Helios,' she blurted out after a slight hesitation. 'He's broken his leg and can't move.' She looked at the shopkeeper. 'Would you please phone for an ambulance and send it up to the Sanctuary?'

'You'd better make haste, Spyros. It'll be dark before very long,' added Daros curtly.

'I'll do it right away.' He disappeared into the back; Daros turned to Jenny, his eyes smouldering, his mouth compressed.

'I w-want to go home,' she stammered, fear bringing tears to the backs of her eyes. 'I have Helios's car so—so I'll use that and bring it back tomorrow. . . .' She scarcely knew what she was saying, since it was not only fear that affected her but also the memory of that scene up there and what had happened as a result, and the drive from the Sanctuary had not been easy. And on top of all this was her anguish that the comfort she craved from Daros was turned to fury against her instead. How she would have loved to be able to fling herself into his arms, to cry out her tension on his shoulder and be calmed by his tender, gentle words, soothed by the caress of his hands. 'If you will stay, just to see that the ambulance is going up there, then I can go.'

She had turned away when she heard his voice rasp out the words, 'You can leave Helios's car where it is. Spyros will see that it is taken to Helios's home.'

'But—'

'Go and get into my car. It's just round the corner; I'll be with you in a few minutes.'

'Daros,' she began, then stopped.

'I have a good deal to say to you,' he gritted, 'and you have a good deal of explaining ahead of you. Now do as I say and wait in the car!'

Chapter Eight

The drive up to the villa took less than five minutes and it was the most nerve-racking five minutes Jenny had ever spent in her life. She tried to gather her thoughts, to rehearse what she would say when Daros questioned her, but it was impossible. She felt close to tears and knew they would come once she was alone in her room. Helios had terrified her, up there in that lonely place, and now Daros was frightening her just as badly, though in a very different way.

He swung the car into the drive, bowled along it, then came to a grinding halt in front of the villa. Jenny looked around as she got unsteadily from the car; there was no sign of life and for this she was thankful. Questions from Sylvia would have reduced her to hysterics, she felt sure.

'Inside,' ordered Daros tightly. 'Into my study. What I have to say to you is not for other ears!'

She went ahead of him, then stood aside for him to open the door. She entered a room she had never been in before. It was comfortable in an austere way, with furnishings of a modern design. The plain green carpet was fitted wall to wall, its colour deeper than the drapes framing the wide, ceiling-high window that looked out onto the terrace and fountain and further to the smooth, perfectly manicured lawn and the shrubbery beyond. The massive desk was of dark oak; the bookshelves were filled with books flaunting bright jackets—except for the top shelf, which was filled with beautiful leather-bound volumes. It was essentially a man's room, devoid of any feminine touch. All this Jenny took in in one brief examination while Daros was closing the door and crossing the room to stand with his back to the window. She looked at him; his face was in shadow so that it appeared darker than ever, and more forbidding.

'How did you come to be up at the Sanctuary with Helios?' he demanded, staring directly at her as if he would make sure she did not lie to him.

'I went to the village for my lunch,' she began when he interrupted her. 'I told you to lunch here, at the villa.'

'Yes, with your father. He went out so I decided to go out too.' To her surprise her voice was steady, but her nerves were stretched and her pulses racing. 'I met Helios in the *cafeneion;* we had lunch together. . . .' Jenny's voice trailed into silence as her fear mounted at his expression. The blood seemed actually to glow beneath the mahogany of his skin. Truly his anger was at its height, yet—for the present at any rate—he was controlling it. It was none the less frightening for all that and her voice was no longer steady as she went on. 'Helios had the afternoon off work, and he offered to take me for a drive, so we went up to the Sanctuary.' She stopped then and the ensuing silence was awful, lasting a long time, with nothing to break it but the quiet ticking of a clock on the wall.

'How,' inquired Daros in a very soft voice, 'did Helios come to break his leg?' The dark metallic eyes flickered over her and only then did she wonder what she looked like, and if the tussle with Helios had left its mark; if so, Daros must have noticed before now—when they were in the shop, in fact. Automatically she lifted a hand to her hair . . . and knew that it had suffered in the struggle. She saw Daros's eyes narrow at her action, the jaw flex and the mouth tighten. Yet his anger seemed out of all proportion, for, after all, she was nothing to him—a guest in his home, nothing more. And she would not have been that had she not chosen to accompany Sylvia. If she had followed her first inclination she would never have come here at all. So his anger was not only illogical but ludicrous.

'I asked you a question,' he reminded her in the same soft voice. 'How did Helios come to break his leg?'

'We had a—a quarrel, sort of,' she managed after a small hesitation, 'and I pushed him and he fell.'

'Why did you push him?'

'He—he— Oh, why don't you mind your own business!' she flared. 'Who do you think you're cross-examining? One of your servants? I shan't answer any more of your questions, so you needn't ask them!'

'He molested you?' Daros gritted his teeth and Jenny felt that if Helios were here at this minute he would certainly wish he had treated her with more respect. Daros seemed even more furious with Helios than he was with her and yet surely he was blaming her more than him?

'He tried to,' she answered with difficulty. 'And that was when I pushed him over.' She stopped rather abruptly, aware that she had answered yet another question, this after she had only just said, quite emphatically, that she wouldn't.

'You've been very fortunate, but I expect you realise that.' He was still in a towering rage but for some incomprehensible reason Jenny felt that relief was pouring through him, the kind of relief that would very soon vanquish his anger. Yet if he thought so little of her, why should his relief be so great? If she had been molested, then naturally he'd have been angry and upset, since she was a guest in his house, but as it would have been her own fault entirely then he would not have had anything to reproach himself for and in consequence he would not have been unduly worried. His manner was too puzzling for her to cope with and she turned away, moving to the door.

'I'm going to my room,' she began when he told her to stay where she was.

'I haven't finished with you yet,' he said

139

roughly. 'I told you to keep away from Helios and you ignored my advice. I am now ordering you to keep away from him—'

'Do you suppose you need to?' she flashed with sarcasm. 'I'm not altogether stupid!'

'Be very careful,' he warned, nostrils flaring. 'Don't try my patience too much, because the way I feel at this moment nothing would afford me greater satisfaction than to box your ears—hard!'

'Why, you—!' She stared at him in disbelief. 'Do you know what you've just said?'

'I told you to be careful,' he snapped. 'Helios has a reputation on this island and I felt it my duty to see that you weren't another of his victims, hence my forbidding you to go out with him. You flouted my advice, and it might have cost you dear!—'

'Be quiet!' she broke in fiercely. 'Do you think I want to be reminded of it?' Her lids had become heavy and to her consternation she felt a tear roll onto her cheek. 'Why don't you leave me alone?' she cried wildly. 'You w-went out with—with Sylvia and—and I was on my own— Oh, I hate you and I'm going home whether it upsets your father or not!' She was almost at the door when he took her wrist and brought her back into the room. She struggled but his grip tightened. 'I said leave me alone!'

'Just calm down, Jenny.' He led her to a chair and put her into it; she stared up at him through lashes that were wet, staggered by the change in him. His face had lost that tinge of crimson, his jaw was less taut and even his mouth seemed to have softened slightly. 'Would you like a drink?'

'No, thank you; as a matter of fact, I had too much at—' Too late she broke off; all the anger surged back into Daros's face.

'You *what!*'

'Nothing; I wasn't thinking what I was saying.'

As if he could not help himself he reached down, brought her to her feet and shook her unmercifully. 'Drinking, at lunch-time,' he thundered after putting her back in the chair. 'Drinking *too much!* Then going up to the Sanctuary with a man like Helios! It's the loneliest place on the island, and you must have known what he took you there for!'

'I didn't,' she cried, the tears rolling freely down her cheeks. 'You know I d-didn't, b-but you just want to—to make me more blameworthy—' A sob choked the rest and in a gesture of total abandon she put her face in her hands and wept bitterly into them. A moment passed before she felt Daros's hands on hers, gently removing them from her face. And when she was brought to her feet this time it was with a gentleness she had known only once before, when they were on the beach in the early hours of the morning.

'Hush,' he said, and it did seem to Jenny that a huskiness affected his throat. 'Don't cry like that—don't, I say!' His voice had sharpened but it was certainly not with anger. She stared up through her tears, sobs still convulsing her body and causing her to speak in jerky tones.

'I w-wish I understood you.'

He held her to him, one hand stroking her hair, the other bringing a handkerchief from his pocket. She looked at it, then went to take it, but he dried her eyes for her and then her pale cheeks.

'I wish I understood you,' she repeated, as if she just had to have an answer.

He shook his head, as if to clear it, and a frown settled on his brow. 'I wish I understood myself,' was his surprising response when at last it came.

'But . . .' Her fingers curled around his arms. 'I think you're sorry you hurt me,' she said, and a faint smile lifted one corner of his mouth.

'Are you perceptive or am I transparent?' was the next surprising thing he said.

'It was a bit of both.' Her pulses had levelled after the shaking and her heartbeats were back to normal. 'I'm sorry I didn't take your advice, Daros.' She hadn't meant to say anything like that at all, but for some reason beyond her comprehension she did not mind burying her pride; in any case, he had buried his, if only a little.

'We'll forget it, Jenny.' His voice was husky, as if he were emotionally affected in some way, and she recalled having had a similar impression before. 'I think you can go to your room now,' he decided, after dabbing her cheeks again with the same gentle touch. 'Rest for a while—and that *is* an order, whether you resent it or not!'

Her expression was meant to convince him that she did not resent it; on the contrary, she was happy at his obvious concern. She smiled at him, her eyes shining and tender, totally unguarded and still misted by the aftermath of her tears. She had no notion of how young she appeared to the dark Greek standing there, so

tall and straight and self-possessed, no idea of
how innocent and artless she looked, her face
raised to his, her small hands playing unconsciously with his handkerchief.

'Off you go,' he said roughly and she obeyed,
her heart singing. The thought did naturally
float through her mind that this feeling of sheer
joy would be only temporary, because, after all,
the chief reason for Daros's concern was that
she was a guest in his house—it must be. Yet she
still could not reconcile the depths of his initial
anger with this particular explanation. However, she was not intending to analyse anything;
she was far too content to enjoy her happiness,
however temporary it might be, for, after all, the
time was *now*.

Sylvia was in the sitting-room when, after
resting on her bed for over an hour, Jenny came
down, dressed for dinner.

'We had a wonderful drive and lunch!' she
exclaimed before Jenny could speak. 'I'm so
happy, darling, because I feel sure I've made a
conquest!'

Ignoring that, Jenny crossed the room and sat
down, revealing dainty ankles above white kid
sandals as she crossed her legs one over the
other. 'I suppose Vienoula will be here by this
time tomorrow. I wonder how she will take to
us.'

Sylvia shrugged her elegant shoulders and
made no answer until she had lighted the cigarette she held between long, tapering fingers.
Jenny looked at her hands, admiring as always
their perfect shape and the exquisite ovals of her

nails. 'She'll have no alternative other than to accept us.' Sylvia inhaled silently, then blew the smoke away from Jenny's direction. 'From what I can gather she's very sophisticated.'

'I wonder how much she knows.'

'Glavcos wrote to her telling her about me—and you, of course,' added Sylvia as an afterthought.

'Then she believes it's Glavcos you want to marry.'

'Well, she's in for a surprise.' Sylvia's attractive voice was casual. 'It's Daros whom little Sylvia here is after, and it looks very much as though he's ready to fall—and heavily!' There was a dreamy gaze in her eyes; she looked all innocence, a young girl in love. . . . Jenny shook her head, wondering how Sylvia would feel were she to give her a full description of those intimate scenes that had occurred between Daros and herself. 'You don't seem particularly interested in my love-affair,' added Sylvia, looking at Jenny with eyes that were as intense as they were curious. 'I thought at one time that you wanted Daros for yourself.'

'I told you, it was only a bit of fun.' She thought of that tender scene of so short a while ago. Daros's temper had flared to the point where he had lost control and ruthlessly shaken her. But afterwards he had been so tender. . . .

'You're too casual about it.' Sylvia looked at her suspiciously as she inhaled deeply and held her breath for a few seconds before allowing the thin blue smoke to escape. 'You were always so averse to idle flirtation.'

144

'Yes,' mused Jenny, 'I was. But I'm beginning to think myself old-fashioned. Everybody flirts today.'

'You're trying to tell me that Daros is flirting with me?' There was a glint in Sylvia's eye and a nasty little curve to her mouth.

'I feel you're too optimistic,' she answered, thinking of what Glavcos had said about Daros making up to Sylvia merely in order to draw her away from his father. But Jenny had pondered the matter since then and although agreeing that this could be true, at the same time she could not overlook the possibility that, on her part, it was a question of the wish being father to the thought.

'I am not being too optimistic,' argued Sylvia. 'I've had enough experience of men to know when one is on the point of proposing marriage.'

Although Jenny frowned, what her stepmother was saying did not make any deep impression on her because the tender scene not long since enacted was still profoundly stamped upon her mind. 'I still believe you're being over-confident,' she said as Sylvia remained silent, expecting some response.

'We shall see.' Sylvia gave a shrug of her sun-bronzed shoulders. They were bare and flawless above an evening gown of blue organza cut daringly low—in glaring contrast to the modest cut of Jenny's leaf-green cotton dress which, though fitting attractively to her curves, revealed nothing that would draw a man's eyes and keep them there.

Before Jenny could say anything Glavcos

came into the room to stand for a long moment staring at the lovely picture of the girl he had wanted to marry.

'Glavcos'—smiled Sylvia at her most alluring—'what have you been doing with yourself all day?'

He smiled faintly and sat down. 'I could ask you the same,' he said. 'Did you have a pleasant time with Daros?'

'Lovely! We drove into the mountains and then had a Greek lunch at a delightful *taverna*.'

'I'm glad you enjoyed yourself.' He seemed far away all at once, withdrawn into himself, and Jenny suspected he was feeling the strain of his condition.

'You were out to lunch, I believe?' asked Sylvia as she took out another cigarette.

'Yes; I was with some friends. We had an excellent meal at the Astir Beach Hotel.' He stared through the window to the gardens, illuminated with powerful lamps of several colours. Following the direction of his gaze, Jenny drew a breath of appreciation at the scene of colour and movement—the fountain like a rainbow, its waters falling into the lighted pool, a mass of hibiscus blossoms exploding against the green of their foliage; a jacaranda tree was pink in the reflected light, an orchid tree brilliant blue.

Glavcos turned and his eyes seemed tired and glazed. He rose from the chair and said, 'Excuse me; I'll be back in a few minutes.'

Frowning, Jenny followed his slow progress to the door.

'Glavcos doesn't look well,' observed Sylvia. 'Perhaps it's something he ate at lunch-time.'

Automatically Jenny shook her head; she wished she could divulge the truth, but she felt she must keep the promise she had made. 'I think he ought to see a doctor,' she could not help saying.

'Oh, it's nothing serious,' casually from Sylvia as she twirled the cigarette between her fingers. 'What were we talking about when he came in? Oh, yes—Daros and me. You don't believe he'll ask me to marry him?' A pause, but Jenny's mind was still on Glavcos and she scarcely heard what her stepmother was saying. However, she did hear the next words, and her eyes widened in surprise that Sylvia should ask the question. 'Have you had any—er—fun with Daros lately?'

The question seemed to have been forced from her and by its very utterance Sylvia had given away the fact that she was still troubled about competition despite her apparent confidence. Jenny paused but, being all woman, she could not resist saying, 'Of course. We have a passionate few minutes now and then. We had an interlude on the beach last night after everyone had gone to bed.' Her voice was casual, but it was inevitable that she should be emotionally affected by her memories.

'I don't believe you, Jenny!'

'It's true, nevertheless. Why should I tell a lie?' Jenny noticed the sudden brightness of Sylvia's eyes and thought that had any other woman been in this situation it would have been sparks of wrath and jealousy that looked out from those baby-blue eyes, but with Sylvia it was self-pity and deep reproach, which naturally made Jenny wonder what her wily stepmother was up to now.

'If it is true,' choked Sylvia, stubbing her cigarette with one hand and seeking for a handkerchief from a concealed pocket with the other, 'then all I can say is that you have no sense of shame or loyalty! After all I've been to—to y-you . . .' The handkerchief was dabbed to her eyes and silence reigned for a few moments. 'I've been friend and mother—'

'Not mother,' intervened Jenny.

'Oh, how can you be so ungrateful!'

'You're far too young,' put in Jenny hastily as she saw the tears in Sylvia's eyes. 'For heaven's sake, Sylvia, don't start to cry!'

'You can't stand it? Well, you deserve to be hurt and made to feel guilty. I've been such a good friend to you, and if you have a spark of feeling for me left in you then you'll admit it.'

Jenny drew a breath, cursing her own stupidity in being moved by what she knew was mainly an act on her stepmother's part. But she did it so well, and as always Jenny was filled with self-blame. If only she had kept her mouth shut instead of being deliberately catty and mentioning that scene on the beach.

'I admit you have been my friend,' she said impatiently on realising that Sylvia, the handkerchief held to her mouth, was awaiting a reply. 'And now can we change the subject?'

'No, we can't,' objected Sylvia pettishly. 'I

want your solemn promise that you'll stop this flirting with Daros.'

'It's not flirting—'

'It is!' cried Sylvia. 'And you know it. Daros is playing with you—but I expect you tempted him!'

'Let's change the subject, Sylvia.'

'Daros—'

'The devil with Daros!' exploded Jenny, incensed, and at that very moment the door swung inwards and he walked into the room, the expression on his face leaving Jenny in no doubt whatsoever about his having heard what she had said. However, he merely looked at her for a long moment without speaking and then, turning to Sylvia, he asked if he could get her a drink.

Jenny bit her lip, furious with herself for the utterance that she did not mean but even more furious with her stepmother for having been the cause of it.

'And you,' said Daros with cold civility after he had handed Sylvia her drink. 'What would you like?'

'A dry sherry, please.' Jenny let her eyes wander across the room. Sylvia had put the handkerchief away; she smiled sweetly and sipped her aperitif.

Was she being smug, wondered Jenny, or was the smile genuine? It was so difficult to tell with Sylvia; she was an expert in the art of simulation and always had been.

Jenny transferred her gaze to Daros, speculating on the paradox of his behaviour towards her—one moment tender and gentle, as if he actually cared about her, then the next moment coldly impersonal, just as he was now. But she could hardly blame him, for he must be wondering what had induced her to utter those words just a couple of hours after what could only be described as a tender, intimate scene. Suddenly she felt miserable, dispirited, because she could see no way of explaining to Daros how the imprecation had come to be voiced. She watched his long, lithe figure crossing the room towards her, and she offered him a smile.

He pointedly ignored it as he said, 'Your drink, Jenny.'

'Thank you.' Her eyes fluttered over to Sylvia again; she was regarding Jenny from above the rim of her glass and now there was definitely a glimmer of amused triumph in the vivid blue eyes.

Jenny was alone on the patio when, at half-past two the following day, Vienoula arrived, earlier than expected, having come from the airport by taxi. Glavcos had gone to take a siesta; Daros had driven Sylvia into the village to get her hair done while he himself did some shopping. He had invited Jenny too but she declined, seeing no sense in wandering around the shops when she had no money to spend. She watched the cab driver take out four pieces of matching luggage from the boot, then carry them up the white marble steps to the front door, which was opened at once by Luciana, whose welcoming smile left Jenny in no doubt about the friendly rapport existing between the pretty

Greek maid and the daughter of her employer. Jenny heard bright words spoken in Greek and noticed the attractiveness of Vienoula's voice, which was faintly high-pitched but musical for all that. A huge diamond ring flashed in the sunlight as she lifted a hand to sweep a few unruly tendrils of dark brown hair from her forehead. Her skin was lighter than that of her brother, but Jenny saw the resemblance in the features at once, Vienoula's profile being etched on the same classical lines and the chin prominent, almost aggressively so. She remembered Daros saying that Vienoula was very independent.

Jenny sat there on the patio after Vienoula had disappeared into the house, wondering whether or not she should go in and introduce herself. It seemed all wrong that Vienoula should arrive and have no one other than the servants to greet her. However, the decision was taken out of her hands within five minutes, for Vienoula appeared on the patio along with Luciana, who introduced the two girls and then went off to make the tea and sandwiches that Vienoula had already ordered.

'So you are Sylvia's stepdaughter?' Vienoula's glance was appraising. 'Father wrote a long letter about you and Sylvia, whom he wants to marry.' She stopped abruptly and sank into a brightly coloured upholstered garden chair. 'How is the affair progressing?' The brown eyes were serious, moving almost restlessly over Jenny's face and figure and even examining her feet, which were clad in dainty white sandals revealing pink-tipped toes.

'You don't mind?' queried Jenny, in surprise.

'About Father getting married?' Vienoula pursed her lips and became thoughtful. 'I haven't given it much consideration; I've got other things on my mind at present.' The tone sounded almost as if a confession were to follow, but all Vienoula said was, 'How is my brother taking it?'

'I'm afraid he doesn't like the idea at all.'

Vienoula grimaced. 'There have been others, you see,' she explained, telling Jenny what she already knew, 'but as they've all been Greek women Daros has managed to deal with them at the outset. From what I gathered from a short letter he sent to me, this affair became quite serious before Daros even met your stepmother.'

'Yes, it did. Glavcos—your father—asked Sylvia to come over and meet his children and then if all had gone well he'd have proposed, but as it is . . .' She was in a quandary, aware as she was that Glavcos no longer wanted to marry Sylvia but sworn to secrecy by the promise he had exacted from her. As for Daros's relationship with Sylvia—well, the least said about that the better. Vienoula would very soon see for herself just what was going on.

'Daros is working on the situation, I expect.' Vienoula laughed. 'And I must say at once, Jenny, that I agree with him in the main because Father's too old for getting married. He ought to retire gracefully and make everything over to Daros, who's been running the business successfully and without Father's help for many years.' She paused but Jenny had nothing to say and after a while she went on. 'There's another aspect, though, which is that everyone has their own life to live, and so who are we to say that Father ought not to marry if he wants to?'

'You wouldn't mind a stepmother?'

'Did you?' Vienoula looked curiously at her before adding, 'You mustn't have been very old when your father remarried.'

'I was seventeen. No, I didn't mind Father's marrying Sylvia; like you, I felt he had his own life to live. Sylvia and I get along very well.' At least they did until recently, mused Jenny, feeling a little sad that a coldness had crept into their relationship.

'Well, it doesn't matter very much to me if Father does decide to get married. You see,' added Vienoula pensively, 'I intend getting married myself as soon as I've finished my studies.'

'Your ring's beautiful,' observed Jenny, eyeing it admiringly. To her surprise a frown appeared on Vienoula's forehead, but she made no comment and silence ensued for a short time while Luciana, who had appeared with the refreshments, set them down on the marble-topped table.

'I'll pour, Luciana, thank you.' With a smile Vienoula dismissed her and lifted the silver teapot, poising it above a cup. 'I take it you will have a drink with me?'

'Of course.'

With the tea poured and passed over, Jenny helped herself to sugar from the matching silver box.

'How is Father?' Vienoula picked up a sandwich and held it in her hand. 'Luciana said he was having a siesta. That's not like him; he's

153

always had lots of energy. He likes pottering about in the garden.'

'It's very hot today,' Jenny pointed out unnecessarily, but just for something to say. How long would Glavcos be able to keep his anxieties from his children? she wondered. The pains in his chest could be serious, the prelude to a heart attack.

'The heat's never bothered him; he's used to it.' Vienoula took a bite from her sandwich. 'How does it affect you?'

'I'm enjoying it.'

'You like our island?'

'It's beautiful. I found some antiquities,' she added, an eagerness creeping into her voice.

'They're to be found on most islands. There haven't been any extensive excavations here owing to lack of funds. Some of us are intending to form a group, getting students in during the summer from the university, and we shall need a leader—a man who is fully experienced. That, we think, might be the problem.'

'I'd love to help on a dig!'

'Perhaps you will. I expect you'll stay if your stepmother marries Father?'

'I—don't know,' murmured Jenny, feeling insincere. She hoped Vienoula would not blame her too much when she learnt the truth. 'Nothing's settled yet, as you know.'

'And we have to accept that Daros might scotch the whole thing?' Vienoula fell silent, eating her sandwiches, and Jenny examined her covertly, admiring the lovely ring again and the long, slender finger it adorned. Vienoula seemed to have everything—looks, wealth and a fiancé who obviously adored her. Jenny let her thoughts stray to Daros; a pain touched her heart and settled there.

'You look sad,' observed Vienoula. 'Something wrong?'

Jenny shook her head. 'It's nothing,' she answered quietly; 'at least, nothing that anyone can put right.' She had no idea why she had added those last few words. Certainly she had no wish either for curiosity or for sympathy.

'Not a love-affair gone wrong, I hope?' said Vienoula, and as she was taking up another sandwich she missed the little start that Jenny gave.

'No,' she returned swiftly, 'nothing like that.' It wasn't a lie, she told herself, for a love-affair could never go wrong unless it had gone right in the first place.

'If it was I'd know just how you feel.'

Jenny frowned, hesitated and then, 'You sound as if—as if . . .' She trailed off into silence, unable to voice the question after all.

'As if mine has gone wrong?' Vienoula's eyes were neither happy nor sad. 'I feel like confiding in someone, and as you might become a sort of stepsister-in-law once removed I feel inclined to—' She broke off, shaking her head. 'Sorry; we're strangers, so why should I trouble you with my problems?' She took up her cup and held it to her lips.

Jenny would never know what made her say, 'Don't worry about troubling me. Talk if you want; it often does so much good.'

'You're nice. Is Sylvia as nice?'

What a question!

'Sylvia is unique,' parried Jenny. 'She has beauty and charm and everything a man can want.'

Vienoula looked at her speculatively. 'Not an answer. However, I shall be meeting her within the next hour, I suppose, since she's only gone down to the village—so Luciana told me.'

'That's correct. She's at the hairdresser's.'

'I think I shall confide,' said Vienoula after she had drunk her tea and poured herself another cup. 'You admired my ring. Well, the man I want to marry isn't the one who gave it to me.'

'No?' There was a rather awed note to Jenny's voice. 'You mean—you want to break your engagement?'

'I intend to. It was arranged by Father and Daros when I was only fourteen years of age, that I should marry Adonis Stratakis, a man thirteen years older than myself. At fourteen you don't argue with those in authority over you, but my mother hated the idea of an arranged marriage. Hers was arranged and I'm sure she and Father were never really happy together. Well, since I have been at the university I've met someone else—Yannis Patakos, who is reading law and who finishes his studies at the end of this year. He's only a year older than I. His people have no money because dowries have had to be found for Yannis's three sisters. Although I'm determined to marry him, I'm not looking forward to the battle I shall be sure to have with my father and brother.'

'But if you love this other man, this Yannis,

156

that's the important thing. Your father and Daros must be made to understand.'

'So you believe in love too?'

'Of course. What is marriage without it?'

'That will be my argument, but it will be swept aside both by my father and by Daros. All they care about is that I marry money.'

'Well, Daros has a nerve and no mistake,' exclaimed Jenny on impulse. 'He calls Sylvia a gold-digger for wanting to marry your father—' Too late she stopped. Vienoula laughed outright at Jenny's expression of dismay.

'That was a slip and no mistake. However, what you say doesn't surprise me. Isn't it just like a man—and especially my brother—to try and force his sister to marry for money and then raise an objection when another woman wants to do the same?'

'The circumstances are rather different,' Jenny was forced to point out in fairness to Daros.

'Nonsense.' Vienoula was determined not to admit to any difference. 'I shall use that as a lever, saying you mentioned—'

'No, please don't,' broke in Jenny urgently. 'He disliked me intensely at first, but now he's changed his opinion, just a little. I wouldn't want him to increase his dislike again, which he would do if he suspected I was, well, aiding and abetting you in your wish to break your engagement.' Her voice quavered as she spoke; she had no idea just how much it gave away to this highly intelligent girl sitting there opposite her, her eyes wide and perceptive.

'I understand,' said Vienoula in a tone deliberately without expression. 'No one wants to be disliked.' She changed the subject, asking Jenny how long they intended staying at the villa.

'It depends on—' Jenny stopped, biting her lip. How difficult everything was! 'I think you'd better ask Sylvia,' she said at length. 'She's the one who makes the decisions.'

'You know,' remarked Vienoula thoughtfully after a while, 'I sense a mystery of some sort.' A statement that left Jenny searching for words.

'You will understand several things within the next day or two,' was all she could find in the end. 'None of it is as straightforward as Sylvia and I thought it would be when we decided to come over here.'

'I see,' murmured Vienoula, but no more was said because at that moment a car was heard coming along the drive. Daros and Sylvia had returned.

Chapter Nine

As Jenny had predicted, it did not take Vienoula long to discover what was going on between her brother and Sylvia. She sought Jenny out on the afternoon of her second day at the villa and said, almost belligerantly, just as if it were Jenny's fault, 'What's the idea? Is your stepmother wanting to marry Father, or Daros?' The brown eyes glinted; it was plain that Vienoula was furiously angry. 'Father must be dreadfully upset! And what is Daros thinking of? Sylvia's not his sort at all!'

'I think,' returned Jenny, 'that you ought to talk to your father. He might enlighten you.'

Vienoula's expression changed, the anger leaving it. 'I suggested there might be a mystery. I wasn't mistaken, was I?'

'It's not a mystery, exactly, but as I said,

things are not as we had expected when we decided to come out here to meet you and Daros.'

'You won't tell me what's going on?'

Jenny shook her head. 'It's none of my business, really.' She paused a moment. 'I feel I ought to go home . . . and yet . . .'

'No—' Vienoula shook her head vigorously. 'We could be friends. Please stay.'

Jenny made no answer and after a moment Vienoula turned away, saying she was going straight to her father to find out what was happening. When next Jenny saw her she learnt that Glavcos had told Vienoula he was no longer interested in marrying Sylvia. But he had made no mention of his anxiety over his health.

'If it isn't just like Father,' exclaimed Vienoula impatiently, 'to change his mind like that! What worries me is that he's hoping for a marriage between Daros and Sylvia.'

'He told you of his hopes?' Jenny looked at her in considerable surprise.

'Yes, he did. And I know he's already told you of them. But he made you promise not to say anything to either Daros or Sylvia.' She paused as Jenny nodded her head. 'He tried to get the same promise out of me but he didn't succeed.'

'It's obvious that you're not happy at the idea of having Sylvia for a sister-in-law.'

'Sylvia is not the woman for my brother!'

'He seems greatly attracted to her.'

Vienoula looked strangely at her but bypassed what she had said. 'I shall speak to my brother about it. I've already said my piece to Father so he knows exactly what my sentiments are on the matter. Daros will too, before very long!' The two girls were in the living-room, a tastefully furnished salon with one complete wall composed of glass doors across which was another set of sliding doors functioning as fly screens. The view was over the immaculate gardens of the villa to the Kyrou private beach and the sea.

'I don't think that Daros will be influenced by you or anyone else,' murmured Jenny, speaking more to herself than to Vienoula.

'Sylvia is mercenary and frivolous! You must surely agree with me?'

Before Jenny could find an answer, the door, which had been ajar, swung open and the woman under discussion swept into the room, her face pained but still lovely, her big blue eyes shadowed and accusing.

'I heard you, Vienoula,' she revealed at once. 'Oh, how can you be so unkind to—to m-me!' A wisp of lace made its inevitable appearance, and was dabbed to one over-bright eye.

'I haven't been unkind to you,' denied Vienoula, disconcerted by Sylvia's entrance. 'I've merely expressed an opinion.'

Sylvia came further into the room, this time moving slowly and with the grace and poise of a queen. 'Would you have minded if I had been going to marry your father?'

Vienoula considered for a space. 'Perhaps not; I don't know. In any case, your question's superfluous since my father is no longer interested in marrying you.'

'He told you?'

'Yes, he did.'

'I had guessed it, of course.'

'Of course; otherwise you'd never have begun making up to my brother. Or didn't you care?' she added as an afterthought. 'Were you so attracted to Daros that you hadn't a thought for my father's feelings?'

'How cruel!' cried Sylvia, sinking into a chair and putting the handkerchief to her quivering lips. 'Daros and I are in love, but you'd deny us happiness just because you don't approve of me.' Sylvia's voice broke on a little sob; Jenny, glancing at Vienoula, saw her bite her lip. It was clear that she was touched by what she encountered in those pathetic blue eyes. Impatient, and unwilling to be affected herself, Jenny excused herself and left the room.

In spite of her doubts regarding Daros's sincerity in his relationship with Sylvia, Jenny found herself beginning to wonder if Glavcos would get his wish after all, for it did seem that there was every possibility of Daros's asking her to marry him. And it would not be surprising, admitted Jenny, albeit with a reluctance that was only to be expected, for as she watched Sylvia swinging across the lawn clad in a bright lapis-blue sun suit, the honey-tan of her skin gleaming in the sunshine, she thought she had never seen a more impressive picture of feminine beauty and perfection in her life. As if aware of being watched, Sylvia glanced over towards where Jenny stood on the terrace and lifted a hand in salute. So smooth, that gait; Sylvia walked as if she had nothing but a cushion of air beneath her dainty little feet.

'You should have come to the beach with me,' declared Sylvia effusively when she reached the place where Jenny was standing. 'It's just wonderful! I adore Greece and never intend to live in England again.'

Jenny frowned and said, the flatness in her tone reflecting her mood, 'What about the house?'

'Oh, that,' airily. 'You can have it, darling; I don't want my share.'

Jenny's heart jerked. Had Daros proposed, then? 'But you must have your share,' she protested, fishing for information. 'You're entitled to it.'

'I shan't be needing it.'

'Daros has—has asked you to—to marry him?' Jenny's stomach muscles felt knotted.

'He will,' declared Sylvia confidently. 'You must have seen how he is with me—especially these past two days.'

Jenny nodded. Daros had been on the beach with Sylvia for the whole of the afternoon yesterday after spending the morning in his study working uninterruptedly until one o'clock; then after dinner they had gone down to the village to see a play being performed by the amateur dramatic society. And today they had been out for lunch again, returning at half-past three when Daros had gone to his study and Sylvia to the beach, where she had lain for an hour, sunbathing.

'I think I shall go home,' said Jenny decisively after a moment of thought. 'I can't leave the house empty any longer.'

'Oh, must you, darling? Oh, well, you know best, Jenny. I shall be sorry to see you go, though. You must come over and visit us just whenever you feel like it.'

I shan't feel like it, declared Jenny, but to herself.

She told Daros of her decision while they were at dinner that evening. She saw him start, then frown, saw Vienoula's eyes narrow and flick to Sylvia, an unreadable expression in their depths.

'You've definitely made up your mind?' Daros was evidently not intending to raise any protest this time and Jenny, who had cherished the hope that he would once again tell her she must stay, felt so desolate that she could have got up and left the table there and then, because her appetite had gone.

'Yes, I have,' she managed, swallowing the terrible lump that had risen in her throat.

'And when do you plan to leave?' Daros's voice was devoid of expression; he was toying absently with a roll on his side plate.

'I think as soon as possible.' Might as well make the break immediately, for the sooner she got away the sooner her hurts would begin to heal. She had been foolish in the extreme to fall in love with Daros, but how did one combat the physical magnetism, the masculine power that he had exerted over her almost from the start?

Vienoula said quietly, 'Don't go home yet, Jenny. We're only just getting to know one another. I'd been hoping we'd become firm friends.' Her dark eyes met those of her brother and she seemed to be admonishing him. He glanced away and his mouth went tight.

'Don't try to influence dear Jenny,' purred Sylvia. 'She knows what she wants, don't you, darling?'

Jenny looked at her glintingly and could have said, 'I know what *you* want!' but controlled the impulse and said instead, 'I feel the house should not be left empty any longer. We have some valuable antiques,' she explained to Vienoula, 'and it isn't safe these days to leave such things lying around in a house that's untenanted.' She hoped she did not sound as dejected as she felt; she had no wish for Daros to guess at the depth of her hurt. Glavcos was frowning slightly but he made no comment; in fact, he had contributed very little to the dinner-time conversation lately and Jenny strongly suspected that he was reaching the stage when he would have to see a doctor, whether his wishes regarding Daros and Sylvia were to materialise or not. Strangely, no one had noticed that he was quiet, so there had been no curiosity as to the reason why.

'So you want Daros to arrange a flight for you?' It was Sylvia who spoke and to Jenny's surprise he threw her a dark glance.

'Yes—' Jenny looked at him, vitally aware even now of his magnetism, his superlative good looks and air of superiority, his arrogance that was an inherent part of his make-up. 'If you would try to get me a flight by the day after tomorrow?'

He said nothing; Vienoula changed the topic abruptly to announce that her fiancé was coming over to Camina the following day.

'He is?' Daros expressed surprise. 'Why didn't you tell me?'

'He phoned about an hour ago.' She fell silent, exchanging a glance with Jenny, which Daros caught.

'You don't sound overly enthusiastic about his visit.'

'What would you like me to do?' his sister inquired almost haughtily. 'Go into raptures?'

Daros's eyes glinted. 'I think we'll not pursue the matter,' he said curtly.

Vienoula merely shrugged her shoulders and concentrated on her food. But Sylvia was curious. 'Surely you're looking forward to seeing your fiancé?'

'Not particularly.'

'I said,' intervened Daros imperiously, 'that we would not pursue the matter.'

Glavcos spoke at last, ignoring his son's injunction as he said, 'Vienoula has confided in me today that she no longer feels herself engaged to Adonis.'

'What!' Daros's dark eyes challenged. 'You're betrothed, and betrothals are not broken in Greece. What is this all about anyway?'

'I've met someone else—' She stopped, interrupted by an authoritative lift of her brother's hand.

'You and I shall talk about it later.' No arguing with that tone, thought Jenny, trying to imagine how Vienoula would manage to stand up to her brother. She had told Jenny only that morning

166

that she intended to do so but had again said she was not looking forward to Daros's reaction.

However, she obviously did stand up to him, because when she saw Jenny at the breakfast table the following morning she wore an air of triumph that it was impossible to ignore and Jenny found herself saying, 'You managed to get your own way, then?'

'Of course. When Adonis comes he will be told at once that we are no longer engaged.'

'Then why let him come?'

'It's too late to stop him. He rang me from London and was getting a flight to Athens at midnight. He changes planes there because he couldn't get a direct flight.'

'He's in London?'

'He's been on a visit to an aunt who is English and he decided to come on here to see me. He lives in Crete.'

'He's going to be upset, I think.'

'Perhaps.' Vienoula looked at her speculatively. 'You agree with what I've done, though.' A statement, and Jenny nodded her head at once.

'Certainly I agree. It would be just as unfair to Adonis as to yourself if you were to marry him.'

'He might not think so because he doesn't expect love.'

'It must be awful!' Jenny shuddered at the thought of an arranged marriage where the girl was forced to take a bridegroom she scarcely knew. It happened all the time in the small Greek villages and on some of the islands where western influence had not yet made itself felt. Glavcos had been telling Jenny of these customs, and she knew that the engagement was solemnised, like the actual marriage, by a church service, and that was the reason why so few were broken.

Although Jenny had asked about Adonis and had been told that he was rich and handsome, she was not prepared for the charming, quiet gentleman who was brought up to the villa at half-past ten the following morning. She and Sylvia were sunbathing on the lawn and no sooner had the young man got out of the car than she heard a low, appreciative 'Ooh . . . what about that!' from her stepmother, who immediately sat up straight in her lounger and seemed totally unable to take her eyes off him. Vienoula came out and brought him over at once to be introduced to Sylvia and Jenny. He looked into Sylvia's big blue eyes and seemed mesmerised by their beauty.

'How do you do?' he murmured. 'I am very pleased to meet you.' His accent was most attractive, his handshake firm and cool. 'You are guests here?' Although he included Jenny his eyes were fixed on Sylvia's face as if he found it impossible to look anywhere else. 'Vienoula told me about you on the phone last evening.'

'How nice to meet you,' purred Sylvia at her most charming. 'You had a pleasant flight?'

'Very smooth, thank you.'

'Are we going inside?' Vienoula smiled at him and took hold of his hand. 'Daros wants to talk to you.'

'He does? What about?' He gave her his attention but not for long. 'I hope I haven't caused any inconvenience by coming like this—without giving you much warning.' His eyes returned to Sylvia and it seemed that a deep sigh escaped him. Jenny, watching the little scene with fascinated eyes, saw him look at Vienoula's engagement ring, keeping his gaze fixed on it for a long moment, then return his attention to Sylvia's face.

He was fascinated by her, thought Jenny, remembering the many occasions when she had seen men look at her stepmother in that particular way. But, somehow, there was a difference in the admiration Adonis was showing to Sylvia . . . and there was certainly a difference in Sylvia's reaction, for instead of being coy and putting on the familiar act of shyness and embarrassment she was meeting his gaze squarely, her lips slightly parted in a smile.

The silence was profound, broken at last by Vienoula's saying, 'Come, Adonis, Daros will be waiting to see you.'

'He is something,' murmured Sylvia when the two were out of earshot. She looked at Jenny. 'Don't you agree that he is rather special?'

'I do.'

'Then why is Vienoula wanting to break her engagement?'

'She isn't in love with him; it's as simple as that.'

Sylvia's eyes became dark and dreamy. 'I can't imagine any girl who has been lucky enough to become engaged to a man like that wanting to give him up.'

'Vienoula had no say at the time the betrothal was arranged.'

'What has that to do with it? I'd not object if someone arranged for me to marry a man like Adonis.'

Jenny shook her head in a gesture of impatience. 'I shall never understand you,' she said. 'First you wanted to marry Glavcos—'

'But only for his money, darling,' interrupted Sylvia. 'I was expecting to be a widow before very long.'

'Then you decided you wanted Daros,' continued Jenny, ignoring the interruption. 'And now—well, it looks as if you prefer Adonis.'

'He was attracted to me—you must have noticed?' Sylvia gave a deep sigh and her eyes wandered towards the house. 'You know, Jen, darling, this could be love at first sight.'

'Love?' Jenny's eyes widened disbelievingly. 'You don't even know what love is,' she declared scathingly.

'You—? Oh, Jenny, how unkind! Of course I know what love is! Do you suppose I have never been in love?'

'You've probably thought you have— a dozen times!'

The lovely blue eyes filled up. 'You're so cruel,' she accused, as she had done so many times before. 'I think it must be your youth; you don't stop to consider before you speak.' Sylvia caught her breath in a little sob and flicked a slender finger across her eye. 'Perhaps you don't realise just how hurtful you can be at times,' she added huskily. 'I suppose I ought to be understanding and give you the benefit of the doubt.'

'For heaven's sake, forget it!' snapped Jenny. 'If you think you can make me feel a heel then you're mistaken! You've been doing it for over two years and I'm becoming immune!' And without giving Sylvia the chance to make any more tearful protests Jenny turned and left her.

Chapter Ten

It was with a feeling of utter desolation that Jenny heard Daros say he had arranged a flight for her. He had been trying for three days to get a cancellation and now he had succeeded. She was to leave at eleven o'clock that night.

'Thank you for all your trouble.' She had been wandering in the garden when he came up to her with the information about the flight; now they were standing by the fountain and Jenny could feel the cool spray on her face.

'Are you going to be all right on your own in that large house?' Daros asked, and Jenny looked up into his dark face and felt that the words had come reluctantly, spoken with a concern he had not wanted to betray.

'It's only for a short time. I'm selling it and

moving into a smaller place. A flat will be best, I think.'

Silence fell; Jenny glanced sideways at him and saw a muscle jerk in his throat.

'Sylvia said something about your getting a job.'

'Yes, I will have to.' She would have moved away but he spoke again.

'What kind of work can you do? According to Sylvia, neither you nor she has ever worked before.'

'I don't know what kind of job I shall get.' Jenny was becoming impatient with questions that she sensed were forced. 'You can't be interested,' she said, and added at once, 'I must go and do my packing.'

He glanced at his wristwatch. 'It's only three o'clock; you have plenty of time—' He broke off abruptly and a frown creased his face. 'If you must pack then don't let me stop you.'

Jenny's heart contracted painfully as she watched him walk away, his long strides eating up the distance between her and the open French window that led to his study.

After standing there for some minutes Jenny went into the villa and to her bedroom, her every action automatic because all life and feeling had gone out of her. She had just put an empty suitcase on the bed when Vienoula knocked, and entered in response to Jenny's quiet 'Come in.'

Vienoula stood looking at the suitcase for what seemed an eternity without speaking. She closed the door eventually and stood with her back to the window. 'Daros has just told me that he's managed to get a cancellation for you.'

'That's right.' Jenny turned away to hide the moisture that had filmed her eyes. 'I'm leaving at eleven tonight.'

'Can I sit down?'

'Of course.'

'Has Sylvia told you that she and Adonis are engaged?'

'Yes, she told me last night.'

'The affair's moved quickly.'

'I believe Sylvia's in love for the first time in her life.'

'I'm sure they'll be very happy.'

'I hope so.'

'Adonis likes the helpless type.'

'Sylvia's not really helpless but she manages to—to . . .'

Jenny allowed her voice to fall away to silence but Vienoula, faintly amused, finished for her. 'She manages to put on an act.' No response from Jenny and she added, an odd inflection in her voice, 'Did you really believe that my brother was attracted to her?'

'He seemed to be.' Jenny went over to the wardrobe and took out some dresses; she stood with them over her arm, looking at Vienoula and wishing she would go. She wanted to be alone, for the effort of talking was too much for her.

'Yet he wasn't in the least upset when Sylvia transferred her attention to Adonis.'

'No, he wasn't.'

'Have you any idea why Daros showed so much interest in your stepmother?'

'Your father suggested it might be that Daros wanted to draw Sylvia away from him—'

'And that's exactly what he was doing,' broke

in Vienoula quietly. 'Daros never thought that much about your stepmother!' She snapped her fingers in a gesture that could only be described as contempt.

'So it would seem,' agreed Jenny without much interest. She put one of the dresses into the case, folding it carefully.

'Daros is no fool. He soon saw that his father was no longer keen on marrying Sylvia.'

'He did?' she asked with sudden interest. 'Then why did he continue to pay Sylvia so much attention?'

'For another reason altogether.'

'Yes?' What was the matter with Vienoula? wondered Jenny. She seemed to be talking for talking's sake and none of it made much sense anyway.

'It never dawned on you why he was paying Sylvia so much attention?' There was an edge of impatience to Vienoula's voice, which only added to Jenny's puzzlement.

'I thought he must be attracted to her. Sylvia's always attracted the men,'' she added reminiscently.

'Daros could never have fallen in love with her.'

'No,' agreed Jenny. 'He isn't capable of love. He told me it isn't necessary in marriage.'

'He did?' curiously and with a disconcerting stare. 'When was this?'

'Oh—er—one evening.'

'You and he were together one evening?'

'We talked, yes.'

'Talked . . .' murmured Vienoula to herself. 'I don't agree that he's incapable of love.'

175

The abrupt veering of the subject brought a crease of puzzlement to Jenny's forehead. 'He said that physical attraction is all that matters.' Jenny fetched more dresses from the wardrobe and laid them on the bed.

'Daros talks a lot of rubbish.'

'He was quite serious.'

'But he didn't mean a word of it.'

In the act of putting one of the dresses into her suitcase Jenny looked up sharply. 'Where is all this leading, Vienoula?' she wanted to know. 'You're acting very strangely and I don't understand why.'

There was a long hesitation before Vienoula spoke, and Jenny gained the impression that she was carefully choosing her words. 'Hasn't it ever struck you that Daros is in love already?'

'In love?' Jenny frowned, her mind anything but clear. 'With whom?'

'With you,' replied Vienoula and Jenny could only stare, quite unable either to comprehend or to articulate any kind of response. 'I mean it,' added Vienoula, smiling faintly as Jenny sank down on the bed, at the same time lifting a hand as if she would prevent Vienoula from saying anything further. 'It was obvious to me, right at the start, that you were in love with him, and I thought he'd be totally blind if he hadn't seen it—'

'He had seen it,' faltered Jenny, scarcely aware of her interruption.

'I know; he told me—'

'Oh, how could he!'

'He wasn't bragging of a conquest, Jenny, so there's no need to adopt this attitude. I had

176

already challenged him about his feelings for you, and although at first he prevaricated I eventually got an admission out of him. But he immediately went on to say that he had no intention of giving up his freedom.'

'I can't believe he loves me.' Jenny shook her head, her mind half-dazed, and yet she was recalling with startling clarity those times when his manner with her had been so gentle that she had felt he must care for her, if only a little.

'I saw it in the way he looked at you when he thought no one was noticing. But although he was fighting his love for you, continuing to go about with Sylvia in order to take his mind off you—and *that* was the reason why he was paying Sylvia so much attention—he found he could not let you go home on the first occasion that you wanted to, so he set about convincing you that it would be an insult to my father.'

'Daros told you all this?'

At the obvious surprise in Jenny's voice, Vienoula said, 'Jenny, you might not think so, but underneath that hard exterior, the arrogance and superiority, there is a very attractive personality. Surely, caring for him the way you do, you've been able to form that impression?'

Jenny nodded at once. 'Yes, I must admit that, at times, I did suspect he was different underneath.' She looked at Vienoula for a moment in silence and then: 'You say he couldn't let me go before, but he's letting me go now.'

'Because he's still determined to keep his freedom.'

Jenny fell into a thoughtful silence for a long moment and then she said, 'I don't know why you've told me all this, Vienoula. If Daros is determined not to—to have me, then what good has it done to let me know he loves me?'

'I don't think you should go home, Jenny.'

'He wants me to.'

'Because he truly believes that once you are out of sight you'll be out of mind.'

'I'm sure he's right,' returned Jenny, tears coming to her eyes. 'When a man like Daros is determined then nothing—just nothing—will make him weaken.' She looked at Vienoula through eyes dark with misery and despair. 'I think I would rather have remained in ignorance, Vienoula. It m-makes it so much worse—knowing he c-cares but wants to forget me . . .'

'Well, it's up to you not to let him forget you,' returned Vienoula firmly. 'Stay and use your charms on him. Flirt with him; let him make love to you. He'll soon abandon the fight—'

'No, Vienoula, I couldn't deliberately set out to get a man like that!'

'Why not? Hunting's fun even when you're not sure of winning. But with you—well, you can't lose if you use the right weapons.'

Jenny stared at her, deciding that the day might dawn when she could look back and see the humour of it all, but for the present her only sensation was one of unhappiness and defeat. 'I can't do it,' she stated and began to pack more of the dresses into her suitcase.

'You're not even going to try?' Vienoula's voice was edged with disappointment.

'It's flattering that you would like me for a sister-in-law, Vienoula, but—no, I'm not going to try.'

'Then you're crazy!'

'Perhaps, but to tell the truth I could never—flirt with Daros, and—and hunt, as you term it.'

Vienoula looked at her and then, exasperated, strode to the door and passed through it.

Dinner that evening was a silent meal, for Glavcos had suffered a heart attack just after lunch and was in the hospital, and although his condition was satisfactory the occurrence had cast a blight on the three people sitting there, none of whom had any appetite at all. Sylvia knew nothing about the attack, for she had gone off with Adonis, who was staying at the villa as the guest of Glavcos. They were having a trip to another island and would not be back until after midnight. Sylvia had shown little or no emotion when saying goodbye to her stepdaughter.

'Are you visiting your father again tonight?' It was Jenny who eventually broke the silence, because it was becoming unbearable. For she had her own tragedy on her mind as well as her concern for Glavcos, about whom she felt guilty, since she ought to have told either Daros or Vienoula of his condition.

'No, they've asked that we leave it until tomorrow,' replied Daros without looking at her. 'He was cheerful enough when we left him a couple of hours ago.'

'I hope he's going to be all right.'

'He's decided to make everything over to Daros,' interposed Vienoula without much expression, 'and to live in Athens with a friend who's the same age and who has a villa that is far too large for him but that he does not want to leave. Father's made the decision and Daros and I have discussed it and decided to make no objection.' Her direct gaze was on Jenny; it was plain that she was telling her that Daros was going to be all on his own once she, Vienoula, was married. 'This friend has some excellent servants,' added Vienoula, 'one of whom was a male nurse at the hospital in Athens until he went to work for Father's friend.'

Jenny said nothing and from then on the meal was eaten in complete silence. It was a relief when it was over and Jenny, having declined to join the other two for coffee, went out to the beach, telling Daros she would be back in plenty of time for him to take her to the airport.

'We must leave here no later than ten o'clock.' Daros looked at his watch. 'It's after nine now.'

'I'll be back,' she said and went out, deliberately avoiding Vienoula's half-accusing gaze. It was plain that she was very upset at the decision Jenny had made.

All was silent and cool on the moonlit beach, and despite her heartache and despair, Jenny was able to savour the peace and tranquillity of her surroundings. Tears were close, though, heavy behind her eyes, and her feet dragged a little because they too seemed too heavy. How long would it take her to forget? she wondered, and decided it would be much, much longer than it would take Daros. He must be very confident of a quick recovery, for otherwise he would not be letting her go. She would get a job, though, and immerse herself in it; then there would be the selling of the house and the removal to a flat.

She would meet new people, make new friends, and eventually forget Daros, and Sylvia, and everyone who had contributed to this unhappy state into which she had been plunged.

It was just after ten o'clock when she and Daros started for the airport. The moon and stars had been blotted out by clouds, and a fine drizzle of rain came down, glistening in the car's headlights. Daros was silent, morose; Jenny wondered how he could be in love with her and yet take her like this to the airport and know she was to fly out of his life forever. Men, she thought, were so much harder than women; they could even be cruel to themselves.

The airport seemed filled with people— holidaymakers, she surmised, going home after a couple of weeks on this island paradise of sun and sea, spectacular mountains and exotic flowers blooming everywhere.

'You needn't come in with me.' Jenny, pale but composed, spoke in tones that were almost haughty. 'I'll say goodbye here, and then—'

'I'll come in with you. You can't manage your luggage.'

She did not argue; let him have his way to the last.

The two suitcases were labelled and about to go through when Jenny heard Daros say, 'There's been a mistake. We want them back.'

'Back?' The immaculately attired girl behind the desk looked inquiringly at him, while Jenny, her heart beginning to hammer in her chest, was unable to move, so weak had her legs become. The man in the line behind her made an impatient utterance as Daros grasped the cases and brought them away from the desk.

'What are you d-doing?' Jenny's voice cracked in the middle, the result of the agonising lump that had risen in her throat. 'Daros . . . please explain . . . don't torture m-me. I have to—to catch my plane . . .'

'Porter!' he called, and a man came at once. Daros took hold of Jenny's arm and shepherded her towards the exit, the porter at their side.

'Daros,' she faltered, 'what—?'

'You're not going home!' He sounded angry and the discordant note in his voice scraped on Jenny's ears . . . but her heart was singing.

'I'm not?' she returned, deciding that this was the best line to take.

'And you darned well knew you wouldn't be, didn't you?'

'No—how could I?' She was still weak on her legs and she stumbled against him as she stepped down the kerb. His arm came about her, strong and comforting and affording her all the reassurance she could have needed.

'Vienoula told you I love you!' The anger was still there and Jenny realised that although Daros was capitulating, owning to himself that he could never let her go out of his life, he was still not quite reconciled to the idea of defeat, of losing forever the freedom he had enjoyed for so long.

Guardedly, she said, 'Vienoula did tell me, yes.'

'And yet you were willing to leave—to go back to England?' They were at the car so Jenny did not answer, but sat inside while the luggage was put into the boot again and Daros had tipped the porter. 'Well?' he said belligerently as he slid into the seat beside her.

'You wanted me to leave.' She was gaining confidence with every moment that passed, because she knew he would never change his mind now. He had burned his boats, made a decision that he would never alter. 'I had to do what you had decided for me.'

The engine was switched on and within seconds they were driving away from the parking area towards the gate. 'What else did Vienoula tell you?' he asked, once they were clear of the airport and bowling along a wide country lane.

'Several things,' she began, then stopped. 'I love you, Daros,' she informed him, then added, 'But of course you've known for some time.'

'What a romantic way to tell a man you love him!'

'But you don't believe in romance; you scoffed at it, if you remember.'

'Remind me to shake you when we get home!'

'Home,' she murmured, ignoring the rest. 'Oh, Daros, is it to be my home?'

'Where else would you be living if you're married to me?' He slowed down to take a dangerous bend.

'What a romantic way to propose to a girl!'

'How did you manage it?' he demanded. 'I had no intention of falling in love.'

'It's something over which you have no control.' The headlights flared, picking up tiny puddles, highlighting poinsettias along the road, capturing dainty moths in their amber glare. 'It just comes upon you.'

'Like a disease!'

Jenny pretended to take umbrage. 'If that's the way you look at it, then why didn't you get immunised?'

He laughed with sheer amusement and every shred of anger dissolved. 'Bear with me, darling,' he pleaded. 'I love you to distraction but I could wring your neck for all that!' He slowed down, drew off to the side of the road and then switched off the engine. The rain had stopped, the clouds disintegrated, and now the soft night sky was spangled with stars and a full argent moon sailed along in their midst. The silence was intense, the air crystal clear; the scent of night-flowering jasmine mingled with the pungent, musky odour of newly watered earth.

'Let's walk.' Daros's words were rough and brief. Jenny slid from the car as he opened the door for her, her pulses leaping with expectation as, after looking down at her for a long, profound moment, he reached out to take her in his arms. Rapture flooded her whole being as he took her lips, sensuously caressing them, his mouth warm and possessive, his roving hands masterfully sliding over her curves. They moved slowly the full length of her back, then up again to cup her face and hold it while his passionate gaze devoured her beauty, taking in the wide, limpid eyes, the delicate contours of her face, the full lips, moving tremulously, irresistibly, and his ardour flared almost to the point of no return as, for the next few erotic minutes, Jenny was swept into a whirlpool of love-making as violent as it was tender. Fighting for breath when at last Daros held her from him, she coloured with embarrassment at the thought of her own abandoned responses. A low laugh escaped him and he bent to kiss her again, gently this time, but masterfully for all that.

'Knowing you as I now do,' he said reflectively at last, 'I expect you have some quite credible explanation for what I overheard when Sylvia was talking about Father's money?'

Jenny coloured. 'I always felt so guilty about that,' she said, and went on to explain. 'I was laughing, I know, and so it must have sounded bad to you. But one always has to laugh at Sylvia, hasn't one?'

'No,' he stated immutably, 'one does not have to laugh at Sylvia. I consider her to be mercenery and entirely without a conscience. Heaven help Adonis—but it serves him right for being taken in so easily. A man of his age should have more sense.'

'I feel they'll be very happy together, and so does Vienoula.'

She saw him shrug, and he made no further comment, being otherwise occupied for the next few minutes. Breathless when he had taken all he wanted with the same familiar possessiveness and mastery, Jenny began to explain something else he had overheard her say.

'Yes,' he cut in before she had finished, 'you'd have sent me to the devil! I'd forgotten all about that!'

'Let me finish, Daros.' She told him how it had

come about and was relieved to see that he saw the funny side of it. After a while he asked how much Vienoula had told her.

'She threatened to tell you everything,' added Daros on a rueful note, 'and, knowing my sister, I expect she carried out her threat.'

Jenny nodded reflectively. 'Yes, she told me just about everything.'

'Everything she knew—or guessed—but I don't suppose she mentioned my jealousy when I realised you knew Helios. And when I learnt of your going up to the Sanctuary with him I could have strangled you— You needn't shiver like that,' he said, but his voice was stern. 'If there's ever anything like that again, though, you'll smart, young lady. What I have I hold, exclusively, and if ever you give me cause for jealousy then you're going to be sorry!'

'You scare me!' she cried, but it was all a pose and he said crushingly, 'Don't come the Sylvia act with me, Jenny. It just won't work!'

Jenny only laughed and received a little shake in punishment.

'I shall never give you the slightest cause for jealousy, dearest,' she said, and now there was a solemn promise in her voice. 'And you . . . please never hurt me in that particular way, will you?'

For answer he drew her tenderly into the protection of his arms and, tilting her head with a gentle hand beneath her chin, he bent his head to claim her lips in a kiss that expressed far more than any verbal promise could have done. Complete trust, she thought, this was what they had in one another; it was the indestructible foundation on which their life's happiness would be built.

'When will you marry me, my darling?' Daros asked after a prolonged interlude that left Jenny gasping and shaking and longing for him with every nerve-cell in her body.

'Whenever you wish,' she returned happily. 'A month?'

'A month?' he repeated, staring down at her in mock astonishment. 'What on earth do we want to wait a month for?'

'Well, I have to do things—get ready . . .' Her voice quivered to a stop. She would marry him tomorrow if it were at all possible. 'My dress, and—and things,' she murmured vaguely.

'There's an excellent dressmaker in the village who will manage a rush job for you,' he said inexorably. 'We shall be married within a week.'

'A week . . . I can't believe it . . .' Her voice broke in the middle and it seemed to Daros that she choked on a little sob.

'Darling—' He looked into her eyes, deep concern in his. 'What is it, my love?'

'Nothing.' She managed a smile, and her eyes, though a trifle misty, were shining nevertheless. 'It's—it's just too much to take in—if you know what I mean?'

'I have a very good idea.' His eyes were filled with tender amusement as he watched her flick away a tear before it fell. 'How very lovely you are,' he whispered huskily, sweeping her into his arms again, claiming her lips, caressing her hair and the soft curves of her throat, covering

187

one small, firm breast with his hand, caressing it tenderly, deliberately teasing it until he coaxed a little moan of ecstasy from her lips. His mouth was light as a butterfly wing against her cheek as he said, in a voice husky with emotion, *'To fengari kay sis einay auraya* . . . You're so adorable in the moonlight. . . .'

ROMANCE THE WAY
IT USED TO BE...
AND COULD BE AGAIN

Contemporary romances for today's women.

Each month, six very special love stories will be yours

from SILHOUETTE.

Look for them wherever books are sold

or order now from the coupon below.

$1.50 each

Silhouette Romance

- -

SILHOUETTE BOOKS, Department SB/1
1230 Avenue of the Americas
New York, NY 10020

Please send me the books I have checked above. I am enclosing
$_____ (please add 50¢ to cover postage and handling for each
order. NYS and NYC residents please add appropriate sales tax).
Send check or money order—no cash or C.O.D.s please. Allow six
weeks for delivery.

NAME_____

ADDRESS_____

CITY_____ STATE/ZIP_____

Silhouette **Romance**

15-Day Free Trial Offer
6 Silhouette Romances

6 Silhouette Romances, free for 15 days! We'll send you 6 new Silhouette Romances to keep for 15 days, absolutely free! If you decide not to keep them, send them back to us. We'll pay the return postage. You pay nothing.

Free Home Delivery. But if you enjoy them as much as we think you will, keep them by paying us the retail price of just $1.50 each. We'll pay all shipping and handling charges. You'll then automatically become a member of the Silhouette Book Club, and will receive 6 more new Silhouette Romances every month and a bill for $9.00. That's the same price you'd pay in the store, but you get the convenience of home delivery.

Read every book we publish. The Silhouette Book Club is the way to make sure you'll be able to receive every new romance we publish.

This offer expires July 31, 1981

READERS' COMMENTS ON SILHOUETTE ROMANCES:

"You give us joy and surprises throughout the books . . . they're the best books I've read."

—J.S.*, Crosby, MN

"Needless to say I am addicted to your books. . . . I love the characters, the settings, the emotions."

—V.D., Plane, TX

"Every one was written with the utmost care. The story of each captures one's interest early in the plot and holds it through until the end."

—P.B., Summersville, WV

"I get so carried away with the books I forget the time."

—L.W., Beltsville, MD

"Silhouette has a great talent for picking winners."

—K.W., Detroit, MI

* names available on request.